No Educator Left Behind
The Art of a Successful Job Hunt

Vince Evans and Clint Corby

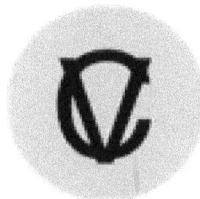

C & V Publishing

Title: No Educator Left Behind:
         The Art of a Successful Job Hunt

ISBN: 978-0-9847484-0-2

Published by: C & V Publishing

Illustrations by Marshall Nienstedt

Book cover by Donnie Hinshaw

Website by Michael Schmidt

This book is dedicated to
Shonda and Heather, for giving us
the best jobs we've ever had.

Chapters

Chapter One

Introduction

Great Blunders In Job Search History

Few know of Columbus's later failed voyages in search of gainful employment. Apparently, not all things are as easy to discover as the New World.

It's a sickening feeling. I've reviewed the numbers time and time again, looking for other answers, but the harsh reality is unavoidable. There is nothing else to cut.

Every school district has a budget that is largely composed of two items. "People" and "Everything Else." People are the most important part of any district. That's why I always strive to hire people that are better than I am. If I can surround myself with quality individuals, then the rest of our goals tend to fall into place.

As I sit here, looking over our ever shrinking budget, I continue to search for something that can be cut from the "Everything Else" pile. The nauseous feeling in my stomach confirms what I already know. The options have ceased to exist. The only items left are obligations that we are bound to fulfill by various government mandates.

The "People" are all that remain. The people. I want to keep every one of them. They are respectable individuals with families of their own. They need this job and we need the skills that they provide, but my hands are tied. People will be let go. It is the reality that we live in. Call it what you will. Recession. Downturn. Economic collapse. By any name, the results are still the same. I will have to release people unwillingly. It is the nature of the beast.

The Board Of Education and I will have to decide how to proceed from here. "What's best for kids?" is no longer the question. As things stand now, it's "What will hurt kids the least?" Education funding goes in cycles. Sometimes jobs are readily available while at other points in time they are scarce. I know that this cycle will end, but at times it seems eternal. We released people last year, people who our students desperately needed. They're gone now. Most have left our community, in all likelihood forever.

This year won't be any easier. In fact, it is shaping up to be worse. I'm off to go scour the budget sheets again for a loophole that I know I won't find. It may be fruitless, but it's easier than thinking about whom I'll have to turn away from my office heartbroken in the near future.

There is no doubt in my mind that sending good people to the ranks of the unemployed is the single worst aspect of my job.

~ Frank, Superintendent

Chapter One: Introduction

Why This Book Is Necessary

"Now joblessness isn't just for philosophy majors."
~ Kent Brockman, The Simpsons

Why is this book necessary? This is a very valid question. However, the fact that you are even reading it right now implies that you are likely in the middle of, or preparing to embark upon, a job search. Our guess is that you have been inadequately trained, if trained at all, for this process. Few universities spend an appropriate amount of time addressing this issue and if it isn't taught there, then where are you to learn it?

In college we (the authors) ended up taking numerous courses that have had little application in our professional lives. Some that come to mind (and we've got the transcripts to prove it) are Racquetball, Horror Movie History, Music Appreciation, Karate, and Calculus (we're still searching for a practical application for integrals), but neither of us ever had a course about getting hired. If you want to know about throwing a roundhouse punch for maximum impact or cliches in 80's horror flicks we can recommend some excellent courses for you. However, if you want to know how to obtain a job, you may need to seek an outside source. Universities are not to blame, they have numerous obligations of their own to fulfill. By reading this book you can take charge of your own learning and gain a true understanding of the job search.

The word "we" in this book will refer to ourselves, the two authors. It is our hope that we can use our perspective to give you an inside look at the hiring process. With this new vantage, you will have a better grasp of what is going on "behind the scenes" and this new angle will provide clarity in the steps to getting hired. We know this book is needed because as school administrators we've seen many applicants commit "job search suicide." We hire new employees for each of our respective districts and have a wide, diverse background that allows us to comment on a number of different situations. We have both worked in some of the smallest districts in our state, as well as the largest. We've also been exposed to urban, rural, impoverished, affluent, diverse, and homogeneous schools, from the perspective of student, teacher, principal, and superintendent.

Throughout this vast array of experiences, we've seen job candidates continue to make mistakes that could have been avoided. They make our choices easy for us by eliminating themselves from contention through their actions (or lack thereof). Separate yourself from these individuals and rise above the masses. The techniques within this book will exponentially increase your odds of obtaining a job.

*"The trouble with unemployment is that the minute you wake
up in the morning you're on the job."*
~ *Slappy White*

Please feel free to read through these chapters in the way that will be most beneficial to you. Skip, skim, and select what will be the most beneficial for your needs. Use the table of contents to locate the portions that are most relevant to you.

Whether you are a recent college graduate, an individual looking for a promotion, an educator who is returning to the field or someone who has been laid off, we have the information needed to help you reach your goals. If you are looking to enter an area outside of education, this book should still fit your needs. Although written by two school administrators the advice given here will prove applicable to most (if not all) fields.

Every chapter will begin with a quick personal story from one of our colleagues or acquaintances that relates to the topic at hand. Some of the stories are funny, some are insightful, and some are simply horrific. Every chapter will conclude with activities and discussion points that can be further explored on our website at www.nelb.info.

Make this book your own. While we believe that everything in this text will pertain to your job search, you have to take control and emphasize the portions that are most personally needed. Next year will you be teaching or still reaching? We're about to equip you with everything you will need to land a job. If you supply the effort, we'll supply the know-how.

Chapter One: Introduction

The Shrinking Job Market Of Today

"A lot of fellows nowadays have a B.A., M.D., or Ph.D. Unfortunately,
they don't have a J.O.B."
~ Fats Domino

This is not a great time to be looking for a job in any field. Education is no exception. School districts everywhere are cutting positions, combining responsibilities and slashing the budget wherever possible. The problem is that a typical school district spends approximately 85% of its funding on personnel. The remaining 15% is often largely untouchable due to government mandates. This means that when a budget shortfall hits and districts are forced to make reductions, positions are ultimately what have to be cut. One study estimates that 275,000 educational jobs are "on the chopping block" in the upcoming school year.[1]

It is a certainty that the balance of power has shifted in recent years. It used to be that one would go to an educational job fair and the teachers held the power. There simply were not enough educators to go around. A number of administrators brought open contracts with them and were ready to hire people on the spot. There was an incentive laden system in place where bonuses were handed out, moving costs were covered and student loans were repaid. It seemed that if you were in demand, you could ask for anything outside of the moon and have it considered.

This is a far cry from the scene today. At recent university job fairs, there have been countless students approaching graduation with looks of desperation in their eyes. Every person has the same questions: "Are you hiring?" and "Will you have any openings?" The power has shifted to the employers. At one point a school would have been lucky to have a handful of applicants for an open position, now they have the benefit of choosing from a multitude of suitors, all hoping to land the same job. In this day and age of the diminishing job market, not only is there an abundance of applicants, but there is an abundance of *overqualified* applicants.

Within recent memory, if we needed to fill an hourly position (custodian, paraprofessional, etc.) we would have had difficulty finding a desirable candidate. Below are two examples to demonstrate just how radically the employment landscape has changed:

- Numerous applications were submitted for a paraprofessional opening (paying approximately nine dollars per hour). Many of these candidates were overqualified (some even had teaching experience). Four individuals were chosen to interview. Two of our candidates were bilingual. One had a master's degree. The other was from the corporate business world. What does this say about the current job market when you can find that crop of talent competing for a job that pays only slightly higher than minimum wage?

- While searching for a new custodian, three applicants were called upon to interview. One had extensive experience as a custodian and the other two had a combination of 50 years of service in the aircraft industry. Both of these gentlemen had made over $30 an hour in their previous line of work and were competing to clean our toilets for the grand sum of $8.50 per hour. You have to bring your "A" game if you want to play in this market.

These are not isolated incidents, either. The current economic climate has dramatically increased the quality and quantity of available applicants. Where we may have had to settle for mediocre candidates in the past, we can now choose from excellence.

The rules of the game have changed. Employers have the advantage now. Applicants have to be more prepared than ever if they hope to be hired.

Activities and Discussion

Welcome to the activities and discussion section for chapter one. Everything you need to participate is located on the website that accompanies this book:

www.nelb.info

It is absolutely free and is provided to you with zero hassle. No cost, no annoying emails and we certainly aren't going to send your information to anyone. You'll need to select a username and password, but that's the extent of the information required.

The website contains an extensive collection of tools to help you during your job hunt. There are sample cover letters, resumes, the Synonym Selector (a resume thesaurus tool), our resume rubric, a chat room for working with other job hunters, additional stories, comics, videos, links to our Facebook and Twitter feeds, consulting services and the largest collection of interview questions on the web.

Every chapter also has activities and discussion topics for our forums. The reason that we have made collaboration available on the forums is because it will make this process a much richer experience for you. If you've ever been a part of a well done book study you know exactly what this means. Don't be afraid to contribute your thoughts and respond to others. You'll only get as much out of the experience as you put into it!

The discussion and activities for chapter one are:

- Go to a search engine and type in "teacher layoffs." Read an article of your choice. Share your findings in the Chapter One Forum in the thread called "Teacher Layoffs."

- What are your strengths and weaknesses at this time? We all have them. What specifically is going to help/hinder you from acquiring a job? Share your thoughts in the Chapter One Forum in the thread called "Strengths and Weaknesses."

* In addition to your own thoughts, you are welcome to respond to the posts of other users. Please make sure to protect the private information of others at all times on our website. Use pseudonyms and eliminate any contact information for individuals referenced. Thank you for your cooperation.

Chapter Two

Prior To The Job Search

GREAT BLUNDERS IN JOB SEARCH HISTORY

Yet another tragic misstep in reference selection.

Recently we had a vacancy in our English department. I began searching through the resumes of potential candidates and decided to contact the references of one promising individual. Upon reaching an administrator that was on the list I said, "Sir, I'm doing a reference check. What can you tell me about Ms. Jones?"

He responded, "Due to district policy I can't discuss that employee with you, but what I can do is discuss the weather."

"The weather?" I asked in a puzzled voice.

"Yes, while I can't talk about that employee I am allowed to talk about the weather. *And let me tell you, the weather sucks.*"

~ Jason, Principal

Chapter Two: Prior To The Job Search
Professionalizing Your Persona

"You moon the wrong person at an office party and suddenly you're not 'professional' any more."
~ Jeff Foxworthy

Every school district implements its screening process differently. Some go to great lengths to examine their candidates, while others don't do as much research as they probably should. Regardless, you should take some simple steps to be prepared, especially those of you who are transitioning from a college lifestyle to that of a working adult. The tips within this section may seem obvious, but questionable decision making is regularly used by job seekers in each of these areas.

- Establish A Professional Email Account

  o Open an email account with a simple and professional address, preferably something related to your name. Employers could immediately move on to the next applicant rather than deal with cuteypie47@email.com.

- Privatize And Professionalize Your Social Networking

  o Making your social networking page available for the world to see is a great way to meet people, keep tabs on your friends, and interact with others, but if prospective employers see a picture of you slamming back drinks at the local pub it will make them think twice about your professionalism. Booze, drugs, provocative photos and inappropriate speech are all frequently visible on social networking sites. All of these can also lead to educators being dismissed from their jobs. They will also prevent job seekers from acquiring an interview.

  But my page is private, so there shouldn't be any issues, right? Think about any recent scandals in the news involving a celebrity. In most situations, they were under the impression that their actions would stay private too. Privatizing your information is a good idea, but both the world and the Internet are not as big as they may seem. If people can't get access to your social networking site, they likely know someone who can. If there is questionable material there and someone is willing to do a little digging, they'll find out about it.

  We're not telling you that you can't use a social network. What we are saying is to use discretion. If there is content on your page that you would not want your mother to see, you certainly wouldn't want it viewed by your potential employer. Use good judgment and when you do get hired (and you will) keep your social network away from work and keep work away from your social network. When the two become intertwined it leads to inevitable drama.

There is a way that social networks can be spun to your advantage. We will address this strategy later. For now, remove the picture of yourself doing a keg stand before it can do any damage.

- Simplify Your Phone

  o Don't let administrators eliminate you from contention simply by your voicemail message.

    "What up? This is T-Wizzle, you heard the beep - ya' know what to do!!!"

    Ah, indeed we do, T-Wizzle. We know to keep looking through resumes and find someone else to call. Keep your voicemail message simple, short, and professional.

    And while we're on the subject of phones, please change your Caller Ringback Tone to a basic ring if you customized it. If you are unaware of what is being referred to, it is a feature where you call someone and hear a song as opposed to a standard ring. When an employer calls you they are not looking for an earful of sappy country music or vulgar gangster rap. A standard ring isn't as exciting as a power ballad, but it is substantially more professional.

Schools want to hire individuals that will represent them in a professional manner. People who lack professionalism are a liability for everyone who surrounds them. Show employers that you are not only an outstanding educator, but an exemplary individual as well.

Ensuring Positive References

"Network continually - 85 percent of all jobs are filled through contacts and personal references."
~ *Brian Tracy*

It is time for a quiz. Don't worry, there's only one question: How can you acquire positive references?

      A) Work hard
      B) Be selfless
      C) Treat people with respect

The correct answer is all of the above. Let's further examine each choice.

A) Work hard. You have a choice each day; do the bare minimum to get by or work hard and be noticed by your supervisor. If the first thing you do at your job each day is walk in and stand around, you are not working to your full potential and people will notice. If you come in and are visibly doing work, including work that no one else wants to do, it will pay dividends. Clean up a mess even if you aren't the custodian, help a colleague in need when they are stuck, go above and beyond everyone's expectations. People enjoy being surrounded by those types of individuals. They are the ones that we remember.

B) Be selfless. You are one small part of a team. People enjoy working with individuals that understand this concept. Make sure your actions are not just beneficial for you, but for the organization as a whole. When you act for the good of the team instead of the good of yourself, everyone reaps the benefits.

C) Treat people with respect. This may sound old fashioned, but when it comes to getting a positive reference this is the most simple and powerful rule to follow. Do you greet people with a smile and a salutation? Do you know the value of "thank you" and "yes sir"? Are you capable of following instructions from a supervisor or are you too busy questioning their directives? Little things go a long way.

When working towards positive references, which people are your essential targets? For starters, you'd better leave a solid impression with your supervisors. But what if you don't like the person? What if you don't agree with their ideas? What if you find them to be incompetent? The answer to all three questions is, *"Too bad."* It's okay to secretly hate your supervisors, but it's not okay for them to hate you. These people are going to be likely references for you. Even if they're not listed on your resume, there's a good chance that they will be contacted. If you think the references listed will be the only ones potential employers will call, think again.

As mentioned in the previous section, this is a small world. We can see who you *want* us to talk to by the references on your resume, but with a little bit of detective work, we can also determine who you may *not* want us to talk to. Whether you like them or not, be a valuable member of the team in your supervisor's eyes. When you are ready to leave your job and move on to a new opportunity, depart with the same grace with which you entered. You don't want to burn bridges with an employer before, during, or after you have worked for them.

For aspiring teachers that are nearing graduation, one of the most vital relationships that can be established is with the supervising classroom teacher. Unfortunately, this relationship regularly ends ups being less than harmonious. This can be for any number of reasons. It may be a difference in beliefs or possibly that the student teacher feels that they can outperform their veteran counterpart. Regardless of the reason, student teachers shouldn't be worried about the actions of their cooperating teacher. They have *no* control over that individual. The only person that any of us can control is *our self*. If you are nearing graduation, be the best student teacher possible. Work your tail off and leave everyone at the building with something extra, something unexpected, something they haven't seen from a student teacher before. Go above and beyond so you will be remembered in a positive light. Student teaching is a unique opportunity to audition for a job. If you bring something to the table that the school cannot live without, then they very well may decide to hire you. Stop worrying about what your cooperating teacher may be lacking and begin considering what else you can contribute.

Working on the relationship with your supervising teacher will be good practice for the future. After all, the chances of you liking *everyone* at your next job are slim to none. However, you *can* get along with everyone at your future job and wherever you may be currently student teaching. This advice isn't just for those approaching graduation. It's for everyone. Get along with your coworkers, especially your supervisors. Work hard and play nice with others. Your reputation *will* precede you; make it a reputation that you're proud of.

Once you have secured a solid relationship with your supervisors, it's a good time to ask them for a letter of reference. In the past, it was common practice that letters of references would be sealed by the author and immediately sent to the prospective district. This is an outdated concept. Unless it is required that they be private (and it almost never is), you want to see your letters of reference. If a reference won't show you what they wrote, find a new one.

The best letters of reference come from your supervisor and list skills you possess. Letters from superiors are not only a necessity, but they are also the most powerful. Letters from coworkers are acceptable and can be beneficial to a lesser extent, but at least one of your letters needs to be from a supervisor. Three letters of reference are usually sufficient, although it is not unheard of for a district to want more. Keep asking until you find three quality samples and then file them away so they will be available when needed. University career services departments can often assist with keeping these on hand so they are readily available.

It is very commendable that you are looking for a job in education, but you will only find one if you can adhere to the practices of hard work, selflessness and respect. Great houses require solid foundations. Careers are the same way.

Activities and Discussion

Welcome to the activities and discussion section for chapter two. Everything you need to participate is located on the website that accompanies this book:

www.nelb.info

- Go to YouTube or Google and type in "teacher fired." How many of your results involve a social network? Watch at least one of the videos that you have found, then go to the Chapter Two Forum and click on the "Social Networking" thread. Discuss what implications this has on a job search.

- Visit a search engine and type in your name. Pretend that you are a potential employer and do a little detective work on yourself. What did you find? Share your thoughts in the Chapter Two Forum thread called "Self Search".

- Who are your references at this point and why? How can you ensure that they are positive? Contribute your thoughts in the Chapter Two Forum thread called "Current References".

* In addition to your own thoughts, you are welcome to respond to the posts of other users. Please make sure to protect the private information of others at all times on our website. Use pseudonyms and eliminate any contact information for individuals referenced. Thank you for your cooperation.

Chapter Three

The Job Search

Great Blunders In Job Search History

The search for the ideal candidate continues.

I am the superintendent of a very small district. I'm not just talking farming community or eight-man football small. The district is *tiny*; six kids in our graduating class kind of tiny. I once heard a person give directions to our town by saying, "Once you hit the middle of nowhere you'll need to keep going for about twenty more miles." Getting qualified candidates to apply can be somewhat difficult. Our pay scale is dwarfed by the larger surrounding districts and many people frown upon living in extremely rural areas.

A few years ago we had an opening and several qualified people applied. One of them was a young woman who was employed by the largest district in the state. She agreed to an interview and asked if a parking pass would be needed upon arriving at the school. I repressed a laugh and told her that she was free to park wherever she would like (our dirt parking lot holds a multitude of options).

On the day of the interview I received a phone call from the young lady. She was curious if she had driven too far, explaining that she had gone by an exit for our town, but did not think it was the right one. She had assumed that there were multiple exits. There are hardly even multiple *people*, much less multiple exits.

When we got back to my office the interview went great. The young lady's only slip up was when she inquired if the principal would be joining us as well. She had failed to realize that I was the superintendent *and* the principal. Regardless, it was apparent that she was a skilled teacher and would be a great addition to our staff. Out of the available candidates, she was the clear choice. But it was also obvious that this particular applicant and a rural community were not going to be the best fit. There was no doubt that she was out of her element. This candidate belonged in the city.

I called her the next day and offered her the job more as a courtesy than anything (I was confident she would turn it down). She said that the visit had been enjoyable, but respectfully declined. There were no hard feelings. The position wasn't for her just like being the principal in a large city would not be for me. We all have our comfort zones and niches. It's just a matter of determining what they are and deciding if we have any interest to venture outside of them.

~ Jennifer, Superintendent

*"If you don't like something change it; if you can't change it,
change the way you think about it."*
~ Mary Engelbreit

We're not going to get too deep with you here. Don't expect any Zen meditation techniques or "Be One With The Job" philosophical statements. With that being said, there is still an immense value to positive thinking throughout the job search process.

You likely have a number of pessimistic people that you have worked with throughout your life, or at the very least you are acquainted with through your personal experiences. Put yourself in the employer's shoes. Are those the type of people that you want to hire and unleash upon your workplace? Of course not. Attitude is contagious; both good and bad, so which would you choose to employ?

We are not exaggerating with the word "contagious," either. A negative attitude is a virus. It spreads like the plague (luckily for us, positive thinking moves just as fast). If you are anything like most people, being around a negative person will zap your energy and your attitude will begin to mimic theirs. As Henry Ford said, "Whether you think you can or whether you think you can't, you're right."

What if you're a naturally pessimistic person? That's fine, but there's no need for anybody else to know. It certainly isn't helping your confidence, poise, or hire-ability.   Hide the glass is half empty persona while at work.

If you apply for a job and you don't hear back from an employer do not be discouraged; you were apparently not supposed to have that position. There is another opening out there that is meant for you. Stay optimistic and remember that without positive thinking nothing great has ever happened or ever will. Your attitude is the dominating factor in your success.

Chapter Three: The Job Search
Finding The Position That Is Right For You

"Choose a job that you love, and you will never have to work a day in your life."
~ Confucius

Every year there are numerous openings in education. Some of these jobs may be an ideal fit for you while others are a clear-cut mismatch. When analyzing openings, you need to be honest with yourself about which is which. In case you need some general guidelines on what to avoid:

- Do you think that eight halves of trig problems are difficult? You aren't an ideal math candidate.

- If you think a megabyte is a description of a hungry man's eating style at the local buffet, consider rethinking a technology position.

- Do you enjoy preaching about Area 51, faked moon landings, and how the U.S. government was responsible for 9/11? Maybe you should leave the history jobs to someone else and hold out for an opening in the conspiracy theory department.

- Is english won of you're most bestest subjects? If you can't be honest about your lack of ability now, someone else will have the unpleasant task of breaking the news to you later.

There is a careful balance here. You need a job and we're going to help you find one, but don't put yourself in a position where you are going to be considered unqualified, incompetent, or both. Personal satisfaction has to be taken into account as well. Can you really see yourself enjoying a job you have to blindly stumble through day after day in a constant state of confusion and unsatisfactory productivity? It's not about holding out for your dream job, but it is important to find a position where you can be successful.

With that being said, you definitely don't want to be too restrictive during your job search. Be flexible and consider your options. Where would you be willing to work and what would you be willing to do? There are nearly four million teaching jobs in the United States alone.[2] The positions are out there, but are you willing to relocate? Just because you commit to a job doesn't mean that you have to spend your entire career there. Two to three years of experience in a position outside of your comfort zone could ultimately be the best move for your career and your own personal growth.

If you are committed to a particular city or area you may have to settle for a position that is not ideal. For example, you may only want to work at school X and teach in the primary grades. However, to acquire a job you might have to teach for school Y at the intermediate level. Flexibility may be a necessity until your ideal job can be obtained.

Ultimately, you can't apply for a job unless it is available, so how does one determine what current openings exist? It's not as if you can get an overview of all the teaching positions that are up for grabs throughout the country by looking in the "Help Wanted" section of your local paper.

If you know a specific district where you want to apply, you should visit their website. Open up a search engine, type the name of the district and follow the appropriate link. On the website, there will likely be a link or tab that will take you to the portion of the site where all openings are viewable. It may be as simple as a button that says "Employment Opportunities" or you may have to search around to find where the jobs are listed. Many district websites have a Human Resources section that will have the information that you are seeking. There should also be instructions for the application process.

For those people who are more flexible and are willing to consider openings over a broader region, nearly every state has a mass application system (you can find all of the links listed at www.nelb.info). This can be utilized to submit credentials to many employers at once. Each state's site has its own unique format; many allow you to apply to multiple school districts at once. The downside to this method is that it robs you of the ability to personalize your cover letter and resume (it will need to be generic enough to be applicable to all districts). Our advice is to individually apply to the districts that you covet most by using the steps on their website. If you don't mind taking a chance on the rest, then cast a line with mass application systems and see if you get any bites.

Job seekers who are looking to increase their options even further can consider private schools, schools in other countries, or even employment outside of education. This practice isn't nearly as uncommon as it once was. One recent study found that approximately twenty percent of workers intend to switch careers within the next two years. Their reasons vary but include interest, pay, career advancement and stability.[3]

We're not telling you that you need to look at moving to a different field or take a position that would leave you unhappy, but we do want to make sure that you are aware that there are numerous options available. Even if it is for a short term basis, there is a great deal that can be learned from working at a "bridge" job while you continue to search for the educational job that is the right fit for you.

"Oh, you hate your job? Why didn't you say so? There's a support group for that.
It's called EVERYBODY, and they meet at the bar."
~ Drew Carey

There are thousands of educational jobs available every year. Is there a position open in the exact school where you want to work? Not likely. If you want a specific job there is a good chance that many other people want it as well. When you begin looking for positions it is important to apply for the jobs you want, however you should also apply for openings that are less personally desirable. There are two reasons to do this:

- Practice. It will give you experience in tailoring cover letters and resumes for a specific job, filling out an application and all of the other steps that go into finding a job. Plus, you may get an interview which will serve as an excellent experience to fine-tune your skills. You wouldn't cater a dinner without trying out the recipe first.

- You have to begin somewhere. Simply because you attend college and obtain a degree does not mean that your dream job is a guarantee. But what if you aren't beginning? What if your position has been cut and you are looking for an opportunity where your career will continue? The same logic applies. Your thirty years of experience does not entitle you to a position of your choosing. When jobs are at a premium, no one is guaranteed employment. We are all expendable. However, you still have the right to attempt to get any job, from the fry cook at a local fast food establishment to the CEO of a Fortune 500 company. You have the right to *attempt*, but you may not have the tools to *obtain*.

Keep an open mind when exploring your options. As college graduates there was one district in our home state where neither of us wanted to work. *One.* During the course of our careers we have both now spent multiple years working for this district. Although neither of us are currently employed there, we both did have a positive experience. It helped to further our development and got us to step out of our comfort zone. If we had closed our minds to the option when it became available, then we would likely not find ourselves in the positions that we have today.

This is not to say that you have to throw yourself into any job simply because it is available. If it is truly going to make you miserable, save your sanity and continue searching for something better. However, by opening your mind and freeing yourself of preconceived notions, you can increase your options tremendously. Just because you don't want to work somewhere does not mean that it isn't where you are supposed to be. Each job you have will give you an important perspective and will prove to be valuable at another point in your career.

Making Connections

"The successful networkers I know, the ones receiving tons of referrals and feeling truly happy about themselves, continually put the other person's needs ahead of their own."
~ *Bob Burg*

The old adage of "It's not what you know, but who you know" holds true in the job hunt. In actuality, it's probably safe to say that it holds truer here than anywhere else. Positions are filled every day based on little more than relationships, families, references, and friendships.

Think about a district where you'd like to work. Do you know anyone that works there? Do you know anyone who knows anyone that works there? You have a large pool of people in your network and the important thing to remember is that each one of them also has a large pool of people. If you put them all together then there is a pool that is big enough that an Olympic caliber swimmer would struggle to cross it. If one of those people drops your name to an administrator that is looking to fill a position, then it might be just the spark you are seeking.

This is also where social networking sites can play to your advantage. Your connections can grow exponentially with this resource. If you are going to utilize this avenue, make sure that your profile page reflects your professionalism. The party pictures that you found so amusing from Friday night will do nothing to impress a potential employer. Neither will misspellings, inappropriate speech, or lewd conduct (see chapter two if you need more specific advice). Aside from standard social networks, there are numerous websites available to educators both old and new where colleagues can meet, share ideas, and relationships can develop. But what other options are there? There are a number of ways that individuals, both new and experienced, can increase their networking reach.

Recent college graduates and aspiring educators can have discussions with their classmates, cooperating teachers, and professors (former and current). Even if this is something you are already doing, ask yourself if you are having the right kind of discussions. Are they specific? Telling your professor, "I'm having a hard time finding a job," may not lead to a productive conversation. But, "I saw there was an opening at Bayside High School. That's an intriguing position. Do you know anyone there that I can talk to?" could push the conversation in the right direction. You will never know the answers to questions you don't ask.

Experienced educators have a wealth of options as well. On top of their friends both in and out of education, there are numerous networking opportunities available at trainings and inservices that take place away from the district. With so many people congregating from different locations the possibilities are immense, but you have to be willing to initiate the contact. Make a point to sit by new people and start a conversation with someone you don't know. You cannot wait for people to approach you and say, "So, are you looking for a new gig?" It isn't going to happen. Having specific conversations is a must. One of those people may have the connection you are looking for. This does not guarantee a job or even an interview, but it does help to get your name out there. Name recognition is important; employers want to hire people with whom they can easily connect.

As your relationships grow, remember that above all else the way that you treat new people is key. If you show them respect and constantly display the best of your abilities, then your reputation will grow alongside your network.

Activities and Discussion

Welcome to the activities and discussion section for chapter three. Everything you need to participate is located on the website that accompanies this book:

www.nelb.info

- Create a list of wants and needs for your new job. Items under "wants" are what you would like to have (maybe you want certain insurance perks, but they aren't a necessity for you). Under "needs" list your nonnegotiable items (maybe there is a certain salary that you require). Post your list in the Chapter Three Forum in the thread "Wants vs. Needs" and compare your thoughts with those of others.

- Find a partner and try the activity called "Positively Powerful" in the Chapter Three Forum. Share your reaction in the Chapter Three Forum within the thread of the same name.

- You have a wide range of people in your network. Write down the names of those individuals who may be useful to contact in your job search. How will you reach them? What specific questions will you ask when you do? Remember, generic conversation is not always enough to get the ball rolling. You may need to make your intent more clear. Share some of the questions you decide upon in the Chapter Three Forum in the thread "Contact Questions".

* In addition to your own thoughts, you are welcome to respond to the posts of other users. Please make sure to protect the private information of others at all times on our website. Use pseudonyms and eliminate any contact information for individuals referenced. Thank you for your cooperation.

Chapter Four

The Cover Letter

Great Blunders In Job Search History

Mixed signals are received from Al Capone's cover letter.

Last year we had several openings at our school and the cover letters and resumes were rolling in. There was a mixed collection of excellent, mediocre, and poor applicants, but one cover letter stood out above the rest (although not in a good way). The letter started off with a standard salutation of "To whom it may concern" but then the author took a different approach. I don't have the exact number of "pleases" correct, but it looked very similar to:

To Whom It May Concern:

Please, please, hire me for this job.

Sincerely,

Jane Doe

The letter certainly was unique. I was curious about the applicant. Not curious in a "I think I'll call her for an interview" sense, but more in a "I wonder when the last time I changed the locks on my doors was" kind of way.

~ Debra, Principal

Chapter Four: The Cover Letter

A Frequently Required Formality

"If opportunity doesn't knock, build a door."
~ *Milton Berle*

Many potential employers will require that a cover letter accompany your resume. They use these documents to weed out the incompetent and find desirable candidates. Your cover letter can move you one step closer to an interview by following these rules:

- Cover Letter Rule #1: One Page Only
  - One page only, no excuses, period. Your life may be exciting, but this is not the time for an autobiography. Get your point across professionally and proficiently.

- Cover Letter Rule #2: Explain Your Intent
  - It may seem obvious, but you need to explain why you have sent your letter/resume. Is it for a specific position? Is it an open application for any spot which you may be qualified?

- Cover Letter Rule #3: Show Your Strengths
  - Briefly explain why you should be considered for the position. What makes you better than your peers? Do you have certain strengths that would make you an ideal fit for the position?

- Cover Letter Rule #4: No Mistakes
  - Eliminate all typos. Don't pick any wacky styles or formats (select a standard 12 point font; this is not the time for a bloated rendition of Wingdings). No cutesy pink paper with polka dots. You want to stand out, but for your professionalism, not your cluelessness.

- Cover Letter Rule #5: Personalize
  - If you take the time to consider the position at hand instead of sending the same generic form letter to each school it will increase your probability of being noticed. One example would be finding the correct person to address the cover letter to. A specific name has a nicer ring than "To Whom It May Concern." If the name isn't available on the district's website, a simple phone call can give you the information in a matter of seconds. Please note that personalizing a

letter does not mean making it overly personal. Do not use a potential employer's first name and make absolutely sure that their title is listed correctly. Dr. Davis should not be Mr. Davis and Mr. James should definitely not be Ms. James.

- Cover Letter Rule #6: Use Quality Writing
  - This may sound like a very obvious rule, but employers constantly receive cover letters that appear as if they were written by a ten year old. Poor sentence structure, inappropriate tenses and bland word use are common mistakes. Some candidates also try to impress with excessive amounts of jargon and buzzwords, but only end up sounding foolish instead. Take your time and write a sound message that comes from the heart. Then find trustworthy editors and revise until your work is polished.

- Cover Letter Rule #7: Make Your Cover Letter And Resume A Matching Set
  - Your cover letter and resume shouldn't look as if they came from two different individuals. They need to work as a team. Use the same font, header and paper (for hard copies).

The following section will provide you with examples to guide your thought process as you construct your own cover letter. With the seven rules that have been presented and the analysis of the samples in the next section, you will have a quality document prepared in no time.

"Researchers at Harvard say that taking a power nap for an hour in the afternoon can totally refresh you. They say that by the time you wake up you'll feel so good, you'll be able to start looking for a new job."

~ Jay Leno

This section contains three sample cover letters from aspiring teachers. Each cover letter is displayed in its original format and is then critiqued. The first one is poorly done, the second is mediocre, and the third is a model cover letter.

Many readers will want more guidance than three sample cover letters can provide. For additional assistance there are more analyzed cover letters in the appendix of this book as well as numerous model cover letters on our website at www.nelb.info.

Cover Letter #1, Tina Jeffery

Tina Jeffery
555 Rural Route E
Anywhere, TN 55501
555-555-1437
tjeffery@email.com

Dear Administrator,

I am seeking a position teaching Art. I am a Highly Qualified certified K-12 Art Teacher. My professional teaching career has led me to travel and experience many cultures, Art, geography, history, and teach students around the world. I have incorporated my adventures and education into providing students with curriculum that introduces them to the amazing natural and global world through Art.

As a K-12 Art teacher, I create lessons that develop a student's natural ability to be innovative and creative. Using discipline based Art Education to develop curriculum, emphasis is on a balance between visual literacy and idea and media exploration. Critical thinking along with other twenty-first century content and skills are developed through hands on project based learning. Art is about fitting things together; images, objects, processes, thoughts, and historical epics. Art lessons help students create with their knowledge; therefore, lessons must include the tools of digital natives. Projects incorporating technological imagery through graphic design, photo journalism, animation, and video are current media of contemporary artists and relevant processes to explore through Art projects.

My professional development path emphasizes working across school curriculum and presenting a global, historical aspect of Art. I bring to the classroom applicable experiences of a working artist and a world traveler. My classroom is managed to instill self-confidence, self-discipline, work ethic, cultural perspective, and right brain deftness. I am a dedicated learner. I continue to set goals and conquer quests. I think I impart this vitality of life to students. I enjoy working with students at all grade levels. Humor, creativity, flexibility, and a genuine interest in students, Art, and teaching are qualities that make me a successful educator.

Please review my resume for an insight into my professional and educational accomplishments and what I can offer your students in learning through Art.

Sincerely,

Tina Jeffery

Analysis of Cover Letter #1, Tina Jeffery

Cover letters and resumes that present copious opinions but few facts are numerous. They can also tend to get bogged down in pointless jargon as candidates attempt to impress with buzzwords and vocabulary. Ms. Jeffery's is a shining example of both mistakes. Let's take a look at her introduction:

> Dear Administrator,
>
> I am seeking a position teaching Art. I am a Highly Qualified certified K-12 Art Teacher. My professional teaching career has led me to travel and experience many cultures, Art, geography, history, and teach students around the world. I have incorporated my adventures and education into providing students with curriculum that introduces them to the amazing natural and global world through Art.

"Dear Administrator" is a weak way to start things off. It's a shame that Ms. Jeffery didn't make the effort to determine who this letter was going to. It's not a task that takes a lot of effort. As pointed out in the previous section, if the information isn't available on the district's website then it is only a phone call away.

The first paragraph is somewhat intriguing; it leaves the reader curious as to where Ms. Jeffery's travels may have taken her. Without any specifics to go by, she may just be blowing her trips to neighboring towns slightly out of proportion. The vagueness here isn't excessive. What *is* bad is the word "Art". Why is it capitalized? Unless it is the name of her dog, "Art" should be "art". Paragraph two pertains to...well...not much at all actually:

> As a K-12 Art teacher, I create lessons that develop a student's natural ability to be innovative and creative. Using discipline based Art Education to develop curriculum, emphasis is on a balance between visual literacy and idea and media exploration. Critical thinking along with other twenty-first century content and skills are developed through hands on project based learning. Art is about fitting things together; images, objects, processes, thoughts, and historical epics. Art lessons help students create with their knowledge; therefore, lessons must include the tools of digital natives. Projects incorporating technological imagery through graphic design, photo journalism, animation, and video are current media of contemporary artists and relevant processes to explore through Art projects.

That was painful. It seems as if Ms. Jeffery typed "Education Jargon" into a search engine and then tried to incorporate all of the results into one paragraph. Some of the sentences are laughable as a result. One example would be:

"Critical thinking along with other twenty-first century content and skills are developed through hands on project based learning."

Seriously? It's like an educational dictionary threw up all over the page. Ms. Jeffery may as well have used: "Cross curricular use of developmentally appropriate zones of proximal development result in learner-centered collaborative groups of higher order thinking especially when utilizing curriculum integration and scaffolding manipulatives." We move away from the excessive buzzwords in the next paragraph, but find ourselves entrenched in an abundance of vagueness:

> My professional development path emphasizes working across school curriculum and presenting a global, historical aspect of Art. I bring to the classroom applicable experiences of a working artist and a world traveler. My classroom is managed to instill self-confidence, self-discipline, work ethic, cultural perspective, and right brain deftness. I am a dedicated learner. I continue to set goals and conquer quests. I think I impart this vitality of life to students. I enjoy working with students at all grade levels. Humor, creativity, flexibility, and a genuine interest in students, Art, and teaching are qualities that make me a successful educator.

The applicant calls herself a "working artist" and a "world traveler"? That's great. Where has she been? What has she done?

She claims her classroom supports "self-confidence, self-discipline, work ethic, cultural perspective, and right brain deftness". Really? How?

Ms. Jeffery says she is a dedicated learner, goal setter, quest conqueror, and vitality imparter, while staying humorous, creative, and flexible. She fails to give actual examples.

Why stop there though? If one is going to make claims with absolutely nothing to back them up there is no limit to the potential. Ms. Jeffery might consider: "I am fun, intelligent, interesting, stupendous, compassionate, ingenious, amazing, revered, worshiped, idolized, god-like, immortal, and stupendous in every conceivable way." The letter then draws to a close with:

> Please review my resume for an insight into my professional and educational accomplishments and what I can offer your students in learning through Art.
>
>
> Sincerely,
>
>
>
> Tina Jeffery

The accompanying resume had better come with some hard facts to back up the claims being made by Ms. Jeffery or else Art will likely be eating generic brand dog food next year. This cover letter does not make the grade and needs to be reworked before it is submitted to anyone.

Erin Mackey
5553 Main Street
Anywhere, Washington 55550
(555) 555-8907
emackey@email.com

January 28, 2011

To Whom It May Concern:

Please accept my letter of application for the seventh grade biology position that is posted on your district website. As demonstrated in my resume, I will graduate from Smith University in May and will immediately be applying for certification so that I will be qualified for this position.

I have student taught at both Gregory Middle School and Wilson Academy in the Carter School District. I believe that the experience has more than prepared me for my first year of teaching.

I hope to have a chance to meet with you in the near future to further discuss my qualifications. Thank you for your time.

Sincerely,

Erin Mackey

Analysis of Cover Letter #2, Erin Mackey

There are no typographical errors or major trouble spots in Ms. Mackey's cover letter. It is grammatically correct and structured appropriately. Still, it lacks punch. While there is nothing to eliminate this candidate from contention, there is also nothing to grab the employer's attention. Let's look closer, starting with the first section:

> To Whom It May Concern:
>
> Please accept my letter of application for the seventh grade biology position that is posted on your district website. As demonstrated in my resume, I will graduate from Smith University in May and will immediately be applying for certification so that I will be qualified for this position.

"To Whom It May Concern" doesn't cut it. Why not take a moment to locate who the letter is going to? Ms. Mackey's competition certainly will.

The opening paragraph identifies the specific position that is desired, so there will be no doubt in the employer's mind. That's a good step. It then clearly states that Ms. Mackey will be certified for the position which should help ease any concern about whether she will be qualified. The next paragraph is dedicated to experience:

> I have student taught at both Gregory Middle School and Wilson Academy in the Carter School District. I believe that the experience has more than prepared me for my first year of teaching.

Ms. Mackey definitely underwhelmed with this section. Maybe she was worried that if she included some specifics here that she would just be repeating what she had to say in her resume. That's okay though. Your resume and cover letter work as a team and they are going to deliver the same message, just in slightly different formats. Ms. Mackey says that she believes the experience has left her prepared for her initial year of teaching. How though? What about that experience made it so worth while? The only thing that Ms. Mackey has shared is the name of the schools. The letter concludes with:

I hope to have a chance to meet with you in the near future to further discuss my qualifications. Thank you for your time.

Sincerely,

Erin Mackey

Once again, no issues, but no flair either. Being concise and to the point is important in cover letters. No one will spend long reading them, so it is an important factor to consider. However, Ms. Mackey shortchanged herself. She never made it apparent why she was the best match for this particular position. She may well get an interview, but her cover letter has done nothing to improve her chances. All it has done is kept her from being eliminated from contention.

Dana Jordan

5055 E. Osage Rd. #B9

Anywhere, AZ 55500

(555) 555-9135

danajordan@email.com

January 5, 2011

Ms. Karan Harding
Washington School District
1000 Central Dr.
Anywhere, AZ 55551

Dear Ms. Harding:

I am pleased to present my resume to you for consideration as an educator with the Washington School District. I am currently a senior at Southwestern State University and will graduate in May of 2011 with a Bachelor of Arts degree in Elementary Education. Upon graduation, I will be certified in Arizona for grades K-6 and have an endorsement to teach middle school mathematics and ESOL.

I recently completed my student teaching Science/Social Studies block with a kindergarten class at Lincoln Elementary in the Roosevelt School District. I was constantly inspired by the progress and enthusiasm of the students in the time that I spent with them. I also had the opportunity to student teach in third grade at Lincoln Elementary in the Roosevelt School District. The majority of my experience, however, has come through working at Allen Elementary School in the Roosevelt School District. I thoroughly enjoyed the freedom I was given as a special education paraprofessional during my four years of employment at Allen. Not only did it give me an opportunity to pay for my schooling, but it was also a challenging environment with high levels of students receiving free and reduced lunches, as well as a student body that was for the large part bilingual. While researching your district I have noticed numerous schools with demographics that clearly resemble the environment I have grown to love at Allen.

I have attached my resume and would welcome the opportunity to meet with you to further discuss why I believe I would be a great addition to the Washington community. I invite you to contact me at (555) 555-9135 or by email at danajordan@email.com at your earliest convenience. Thank you for your time and consideration.

Sincerely,

Dana Jordan

Analysis of Cover Letter #3, Dana Jordan

This is a very well crafted example of what a cover letter should look like. It is typo free, easy on the eyes and shares the necessary information in an easy to read manner. Ms. Jordan found the correct person to address the cover letter to, so let's skip ahead to the first paragraph:

> I am pleased to present my resume to you for consideration as an educator with the Washington School District. I am currently a senior at Southwestern State University and will graduate in May of 2011 with a Bachelor of Arts degree in Elementary Education. Upon graduation, I will be certified in Arizona for grades K-6 and have an endorsement to teach middle school mathematics and ESOL.

Even though she will be a brand new teacher, Ms. Jordan has put in the effort to gain other endorsements to accompany her degree. The amount of work that is required to obtain these endorsements differs by state, but they are an outstanding supplement to anyone's credentials. The next paragraph discusses experience:

> I recently completed my student teaching Science/Social Studies block with a kindergarten class at Lincoln Elementary in the Roosevelt School District. I was constantly inspired by the progress and enthusiasm of the students in the time that I spent with them. I also had the opportunity to student teach in third grade at Lincoln Elementary in the Roosevelt School District. The majority of my experience, however, has come through working at Allen Elementary School in the Roosevelt School District. I thoroughly enjoyed the freedom I was given as a special education paraprofessional during my four years of employment at Allen. Not only did it give me an opportunity to pay for my schooling, but it was also a challenging environment with high levels of students receiving free and reduced lunches, as well as a student body that was for the large part bilingual. While researching your district I have noticed numerous schools with demographics that clearly resemble the environment I have grown to love at Allen.

In addition to her student teaching there is authentic experience to support Ms. Jordan here. Many candidates looking to obtain a teaching job look down upon the prospect of working as a paraprofessional, but it is hard work and invaluable experience. Plus it offers the opportunity to see numerous different educators at work so a wealth of ideas can be collected.

Ms. Jordan even takes the time to specifically tailor her cover letter towards the Washington School District. She points out that the school she has been working for bears a close resemblance to some Washington schools. Ms. Jordan then finishes with a closing paragraph:

I have attached my resume and would welcome the opportunity to meet with you to further discuss why I believe I would be a great addition to the Washington community. I invite you to contact me at (555) 555-9135 or by email at danajordan@email.com at your earliest convenience. Thank you for your time and consideration.

This cover letter was solid throughout. There was no meandering as the document had a very clear structure and purpose. Paragraph one was for education, paragraph two was for experience, and paragraph three restated contact information. This is a cover letter that is worthy of an interview.

Welcome to the activities and discussion section for chapter four. Everything you need to participate is located on the website that accompanies this book:

www.nelb.info

- Post your cover letter in the Chapter Four Forum in the thread "Cover Letters". Give constructive feedback to at least one other user who has posted a cover letter.

- One of the ways to increase the effectiveness of your cover letter is to add personal touches and individualize it (discussing your abilities in Spanish when submitting to a school with a high population of Spanish speakers, for example). In the Chapter Four Forum click on the "Cover Letter Personalization" thread and discuss some ways that you have managed to accomplish this task.

* In addition to your own thoughts, you are welcome to respond to the posts of other users. Please make sure to protect the private information of others at all times on our website. Use pseudonyms and eliminate any contact information for individuals referenced. Thank you for your cooperation.

Chapter Five

Resumes And Applications

Amelia hopes that her vocabulary skills will make
up for her inability to read a compass.

"Can I have the job?"

I couldn't believe what I had just heard, but since she was still standing there in anticipation, it was clear that my ears had not deceived me. I informed the substitute teacher who had just barged through my door that, no, it was not that simple.

We had just posted a job opening online that morning and Anne, one of our regular substitutes, saw the vacancy during her plan time. She then decided that her best course of action was to fly into my office unannounced and ask to be hired. This was not a humorous inquiry either; Anne is not a joker. Somehow, she had gotten it into her head that this was the appropriate way to land the gig. No application, no resume, no interview; Anne assumed that the job was on an "ask and ye shall receive" basis. That is one of the reasons why Anne is still a substitute teacher.

I've seen a lot of desperate attempts to get hired in my time as principal. Poor judgment is regularly on display when it comes to desperate job seekers. Applicants have harassed me with phone calls, dropped by for uninvited "interviews", and bludgeoned me with repeated emails. Anne stands above the rest. What did she think I was going to say? I can only guess that with her warped sense of judgment she assumed my response would be, "Yes, when can you start?" Instead, I sent her on her way, shook my head, and made a mental note that Anne would never work for us in a full time capacity. This job is difficult enough without hiring clueless people that will create additional problems. Applicants will go through the proper steps and they'll do so in a professional fashion. Applications, cover letters, resumes and references are there for a reason.   If applicants choose to make their own rules, especially rules which seem to defy all logic, then they'll be searching elsewhere for work.

~ Natalie, Principal

Successful Resume Strategies

"This resume is like a lonely guy who can't get a date, so he sits at home and eats and gets bigger and bigger. I meet people all the time who think employers are going to get excited by lots of detail in their resumes. No. Instead, [employers] think, 'Here's a guy who can't prioritize and who doesn't respect his reader.'"
~ Mark Nelson

There is not one set way to create your resume. A number of different styles and techniques exist, but ultimately you will need to select what works best for you. Keep in mind that an immediate impact needs to be made on whoever is viewing it. Administrators will only briefly examine each resume, so yours needs to instill the reader with a desire to learn more about you. The following tips should help guide your decision making process. We've divided our advice into two separate categories: structure and wording.

Category One: Structure

- **Required Headings**

  There are three necessary headings in your resume: education, experience and references. We'll explore education and experience now, while references will be discussed in the next section.

  o *Education* - You're a professional, so make sure it appears that way. Employers don't want to know about your high school or the junior college where you acquired twelve credit hours. That's not meant to be a knock against junior colleges, but the information isn't relevant unless you acquired a degree. The only exception would be if you are an alumnus of the particular high school or junior college to which you are applying. Employers enjoy the familiarity of a recognizable candidate.

  o *Experience* - Only list jobs that will present you in a positive light. If you worked somewhere for three months, why put it on your resume? Even if you left for perfectly logical reasons, it will still appear as if you are job hopping. Relevance is a factor to consider as well. Your experience as a sixteen year old at the local burger joint does not typically factor into an employer's decision on whether or not you will make an effective second grade teacher. However, that's not to say that there aren't exceptions to the rule. If you are coming fresh out of college, and put in a solid four years at a grocery store to help pay the bills, list it proudly. Employers like knowing when someone isn't scared of an honest day's work and can hold down a job for a sustained period of time. Plus, there are an amazing amount of skills that transfer to other jobs, even if they seem unrelated on the surface. For example, the people skills that can be developed from working at a business will readily apply to the educational field; all jobs require effective communication.

- **List Your Certifications**

    If your certifications are not clearly indicated under your "Education" heading, then you need to have a separate section where they are listed. No administrator wants to bring in a candidate that may not be qualified for the job. Leave no doubt in their mind.

- **Stand Out**

    What is going to make your resume stand out from the rest? One thing to consider is that there are good and bad varieties of standing out. If you submit your resume in horizontal format on neon green paper in 48 point font it will certainly garner some attention, just not the kind you want. However, if your resume looks the same as everyone else's, it will get you nowhere. So how can you stand out in a positive fashion? Some options are:

    o *Community Service* - If you helped a little old lady cross the street once when you were twelve, it isn't a resume worthy act. If you have authentic experience and are regularly involved in volunteerism, it can be eye catching to an employer.

    o *Bilingualism* - Your week long vacation in Cancun does not qualify you as a Spanish speaker (no matter how well you can say "margarita"). Surprisingly though, people with real second language capabilities fail to list them on resumes. If you know multiple languages it speaks volumes about you, so make sure to list it.

    o *Published Works* - A contribution to the comments section on your local newspaper's website won't qualify. Books certainly do and articles for magazines, respected blogs and websites can be intriguing. Use good judgment and choose what will advance your chances and what won't.

    o *Awards* - "Most Likely To Be Imprisoned" from your high school yearbook does nothing to advance your credibility. "Teacher Of The Year" most certainly does.

o *Websites Created* - If they are fine tuned and of appropriate content it says a great deal about your tech savvy. Avoid the dirty joke site that you've been working on, but do include the lesson plan resource web page that you've poured your efforts into.

o *Customization* - There is nothing that says that your resume has to be the same for every district. Specific items that will increase your probability of receiving an interview for a particular job should be listed. For example, if a school district is in need of a new volleyball coach and you played college volleyball, make sure that finds its way onto your resume.

o *Activities* – If an employer sees that you have experience coaching or sponsoring an activity it may appeal to them (especially if they have a need in that area). Athletics, debate, drama, newspaper and yearbook are but a few examples. Involvement in committees can also have the same effect.

- ***Increase Your Resume's Readability***

A font size of 10 to 12 is acceptable on your resume. Typically it won't be a teenager examining your credentials. Take mercy on those older eyes and maybe they will return the favor. As for font type, select something that is easy to read and professional. We recommend that you choose a Serif or Sans Serif font. Some acceptable ones to consider are:

Serif	*Sans Serif*
Bell MT	Arial
Bodoni	Franklin Gothic
Georgia	Gill Sans
Times New Roman	Verdana

Using different fonts for the headings and body of your resume is fine, just don't get carried away. Select one or two fonts for the entire document and be consistent (if you use Arial for a heading, use Arial for *all* of your headings). Anything else will leave your resume looking as if it has been edited by a first grader who has discovered a word processor for the first time.

- *Eliminate Unnecessary Information*

What would you think if you were trying to hire an employee and saw bulleted items under their experience as "Teacher" that read:

- Created Lesson Plans
- Monitored Students
- Managed Classroom Behaviors

This filler is completely unnecessary. If you're going to list those items then why not include:

- Eating
- Breathing
- Sleeping

Why do people feel the need to list obvious tasks on their resumes? Often it is because they don't think they have any other experience that is worth mentioning. That is understandable, but seriously, will "Created Lesson Plans" get a candidate through the door for an interview? Even if you're grasping for straws, there has to be something more unique that can make your resume "pop". Consider:

- Unique Aspects of Your Former/Current Schools (High rates of poverty/ESOL Students/etc.)
- Presentations
- Training
- Committees
- Leadership Experiences
- Extra Involvement (Employers want to see that you are someone who gets involved, instead of coming and going with the bell)

- *Keep Your Margins Standard*

Don't get overly creative. Whatever the margins are set at when you open up a word processing document is fine; there is no need to reinvent the wheel. Somewhere from half an inch to a full inch will work fine. Anything outside of that range will look odd. When creating indents in a resume, use the tab key, *not* the space bar. This will keep everything aligned properly.

- *Standardize Your Bullets*

  - o pick one type of bullet
  - b) and stick with it
  - ➤ throughout your resume
  - ❖ numerous types of bullets
    - ▪ with odd spacing
- will make employers
  - • question your judgment

- *Be Consistent*

  Bullets, fonts and spacing aren't the only things that should be consistent throughout your resume. Create uniformity when using:

  - o *Dates* – Do not list dates chronologically in one portion of the resume and reverse chronologically in another. Pick what best highlights your accomplishments (typically the most recent activity you have accomplished should go first; you will have to be the judge of which style puts your most relevant and meaningful work at the top of the list) and stick with that style throughout. Also, write dates consistently. Do not use 5/1/09 in one section and May 5, 2009 in another.

  - o *Abbreviations* – If you use UT in one portion of your resume, don't write out Utah in another. Pick one and stick with it.

  - o *Caps* – If you have chosen to capitalize every word in bulleted lists, do so for the entire resume.

  - o *Text Features* – Make sure that the rules you follow for bold, italicized and underlined words remain consistent.

- *Be Brief*

  How long should a resume be? One page? Two? More? There are many determining factors that dictate the length of your resume, but rest assured that erring on the side of brevity is the way to go.

  We've seen some amazing missteps on resume length. Brand new teachers and those with only a year or two of experience under their belt have submitted five and six page monstrosities. This is an effective technique to move your resume from an employer's hand to the trash. It's ridiculous to think that you need a resume of that length at any point in your life, much less when your career is just getting started.

Our personal resumes have typically fluctuated between one and two pages with an additional page for references. The length varied depending on what the job was and what information needed to be shared.

The true purpose of a resume is to acquire an interview. What type of document will accomplish that task? In our opinion, it is a short, powerful, concise resume. It shouldn't be a long drawn out document, crammed with filler and wasted space. It should be so eye catching it demands that you be interviewed. School administrators are incredibly busy people and there is only one opportunity to make a first impression upon them. If your resume is structured correctly, it will dramatically improve your chances of obtaining an interview.

- ***Use White Space To Your Advantage***

It's simple, but true. If your resume looks like an excerpt from the latest John Grisham novel, no one wants to read it. Find a nice balance, and make it appealing to the eye. Forget all about the words for a moment and look at the page as a whole. Is it *"Ahh"* or *"Blah"*? Don't have an eye for aesthetics? Find someone who does.

Category Two: Wording

- ***Avoid Run On Sentences***

We've already discussed the importance of being brief in regard to the entire resume, but there is something to be said for brevity in individual sentences too because if you keep a sentence going for ever and ever and never give the reader a chance to come up for air it can become quite tedious and leaves your writing with a very amateur feel and we don't want that when we're trying to show everyone what a professional you are because it will definitely hurt your chances of being hired and that would be awful so let's agree not to have run on sentences especially since they are quite annoying, don't you think?

- *Eliminate Typos*

  Guess where resumes/applications with typos end up? That's right. Straight in the garbage. Just this year a woman with extensive experience and a doctorate from a respectable university applied for a position at one of our schools. There were three separate typos on her resume. It went in the trash. If you can't take the time to edit your work, then what else can't/won't you do?

- *Have An Editor*

  Find someone you trust (or better yet, multiple someones) and make sure that they know correct grammar inside and out. You also need to select someone who will be honest with you. If you have written something on your resume that will lessen your chances of getting hired, the person needs to be comfortable telling you and you need to be comfortable hearing it. Your sweet grandmother saying, "This looks wonderful dear, they're bound to hire you!" isn't constructive enough criticism to get the job done.

- *Use Powerful Wording*

  Your resume needs powerful vocabulary; finding the proper words to highlight your experience can separate you from the rest of the pack. "Planned math lessons" could be replaced with "Implemented math instruction that specifically targeted state standards".

  You can use a thesaurus if your wordage needs a boost. If you would like a resource that specifically targets resumes, we have created a tool to help you with this process. It is called the Synonym Selector and it will give you more substantial and powerful replacements for common resume words. You can find it in the appendix, or on our website under "Resources" at: www.nelb.info

  Please note that "powerful wording" does not mean including every bit of educational jargon you can find in an attempt to sound knowledgeable. You want to sound respectable, not ridiculous. The Synonym Selector should help you to accomplish this.

- *Avoid "I"*

  It is common practice to avoid using the word "I" when writing a resume. This is easier than it sounds. We'll share examples of resumes without "I" in this chapter as well as in the appendix and on our website.

- *Use Appropriate And Consistent Tenses*

  Are you writing about your current job? Then you *teach* students. If it is a past job then you *taught* students. Pick the right tense for what you are explaining and stick with it.

- *Clarify Acronyms*

  Keep your ADD in check ASAP or we may have to refer you to the CST for a possible AIP or IEP (depending on the ETR you may only need a SIP). Is that sentence making you feel a little DD? It may do the same to potential employers, so spell out any acronyms that could be in doubt. We can figure out that the RI in Providence, RI stands for Rhode Island. However, to assume that we know that MNWSSCC stands for Mid Northwestern Saskatchewan State Community College may be an error in judgment.

  Many people assume that acronyms are nationwide, when in fact, they may only be understood locally. If you are unsure, enter the acronym into a search engine and see what happens. If it results in hits from all over the country, then you're in good shape. If all the information shown is from your state or district then you need to clarify what you are talking about and avoid a chance of obscurity.

Ultimately, you need to go with your instincts. If you think it might be a mistake to put something on your resume, it likely is. Go with your gut, have someone with experience look it over, polish it to perfection, and you should be fine.

If that doesn't work and it becomes apparent that you are not capable of constructing a quality resume by yourself, seek help. There are resume templates on Microsoft Word that can assist you if starting from scratch is proving problematic. If there are other issues, then you likely have skilled peers who can help you with this task. There are also professionals you can hire to craft a quality resume for you. We offer this service to those who are interested (check our website for additional details).

The hardest thing to learn in life is which bridge to cross and which to burn.
~ David Russell

As was pointed out earlier in chapter two, you certainly don't want to list a reference on your resume that is going to give you a less than desirable review. You also want your references to know that you are listing them so they are prepared. It can be very disconcerting when a reference is contacted and they can't place the applicant. Also troubling is when an employer is called for a reference check on one of their staff members and they have no clue that the individual is searching for a new job.

These issues happen because of a lack of preparation and forethought on the applicant's part. Make sure to talk with your references before a potential employer does. If you get a feeling upon talking to them that the person may not give you a good reference, then replace them with someone who will.

Also discussed in chapter two was the need to make sure to select supervisors as references (coworkers are acceptable to include, but supervisors are a must). Did you have multiple supervisors at your last job? Select the one with which you had the best working relationship. Steer clear of personal references (unless specifically requested). We are sure that your mom finds you to be very sweet, caring, and compassionate, but employers have no desire to talk to her about your professional qualifications. Select people that you can count on for a true opinion of how you handle your craft.

One other thing to consider is that if your references are "known" it can be a big break for you. For example, let's say that Mrs. X is the superintendent of a district you would like to work for. If you know that Mrs. X is friends with your colleague Mr. Y, then Mr. Y could be an outstanding reference for you (assuming that you get along with Mr. Y and he thinks highly of your work). Mrs. X will likely catch his name on your references and will inquire about you. There are also references that stand out because they are known, but not on a personal level. We've called famous coaches, well known politicians, and local celebrities when they show up on a reference list. It's intriguing.   Curiosity gets the better of us and we wonder if the applicant's connection to the reference is legitimate (plus it is an opportunity to chat with someone outside of our normal circle).

There has been a debate for some time now about whether applicants should list references on resumes. It is our opinion that this debate needs to come to a close. References *should* be listed on your resume. We despise seeing "References Upon Request" or any other variation of it. The statement will hinder your chances of receiving a job at our schools. What it says to us is:

- o I'm too lazy to do this portion of my resume right now. If you want to do some extra work and call me about references then I'll consider sharing them.

- o I'm hiding something. I can't list three people that have good things to say about me because I don't know three people that have been impressed with my abilities.

- o I have not asked for references and my employer does not know I am looking for a new job. I'm considering bailing on them abruptly and might do the same to you in the future if given an opportunity.

- o My time is more important than your time.

People are busy. They have no desire to call you and ask for your references. If you are hiding something, they are likely going to find out. Rest assured that good employers will call your references whether you like it or not.

So what is the misconceived rationale behind not including your references? There are a number of wild reasons that can be uncovered with a quick search of the web:

- *"I don't want to bother my references by having them get a lot of phone calls."* If you're scared that your references are going to get annoyed with helping you, then they probably aren't the best choice anyway. We know that our references hold us in high regard and are willing to put in the work to help us. If you can't say the same, then you may want to reconsider your selections.

- *"They're going to ask for them on the application anyway."* True, they probably will, but what makes you think employers are even going to look at your application? Many of the administrators we know examine resumes first, meaning that numerous applications are never even seen. What if you had an eye catching reference (such as someone the employer knows) that could have landed you an interview?

- *"Employers will ask for your references during the interview."* Yes they might, but should they have to? Your mom had to ask you to pick up your room when you were a kid, but only when you didn't do it first. Why would you want to intentionally create extra work for a potential employer?

- *"What if I decide I don't want the job? I don't want them to still be calling my references."* Yes, that would be awful, wouldn't it? What would happen if those extra phone calls were made?!?! Not phone calls, *anything but phone calls!* The implications are horrific!

- *"If I add another page it will make my resume too long."* We're sticklers for resume length, too. One or two pages is the limit in our opinion, but that's one to two pages *not including your references.* They don't count against you. No employer is going to look at an additional page with three to five names and contact information and say, *"Nope, they crossed the threshold. Those names really tick me off, this one is out of the running!"*

After talking to a large collection of employers and scouring the Internet we found *one* justifiable rationale for excluding references on a resume. If you haven't supplied your references and they are asked for during an interview, it will give you time to contact them before your potential employer. Contacting them will allow you to discuss the specifics of what makes you a great fit for that specific job. It will give them talking points if they are called. We can see how this may be helpful, but couldn't you also call your references prior to your interview to give them a heads up on the situation? It's true that this may not be possible if the employer beats you to the punch, but we do not see this rationale being a justifiable reason to omit references. This one possible exception is massively outweighed by the opposing factors.

Include your references and list them in a consistent manner. Make sure to include where they can be reached. You do not want to list a phone number for one individual, while excluding it from another. If you need a separate page, that is perfectly acceptable. Sample references are available on the resumes in the following section.

"What is it that you like doing? If you don't like it, get out of it, because you will be lousy at it."
~ Lee Iacocca

What follows are three sample resumes. One is poor, one is mediocre and one is a model resume. These are based on real resumes that were submitted to school districts (the names and locations have been changed). Each resume is displayed in its original format and is then analyzed and critiqued by the use of our Resume Rubric. The rubric will help demonstrate which resumes will end up in the trash, which will be considered and which will result in an interview.

To provide additional assistance to you there are three more analyzed resumes in the appendix. There are also numerous examples of model resumes available on our website at www.nelb.info. While the three resumes here are from aspiring teachers looking for their first educational job, the resumes in the appendix and online cover a wide array of candidates from different backgrounds seeking a variety of employment opportunities.

Karl Turgen
2872 27th Rd, Anywhere, California 55555
kturgen@email.com ♦ Residence: (555) 555–2457 ♦ Cellular: (555) 555-6602

STUDENT-FOCUSED PHYSICAL EDUCATION TEACHER
Reflective teacher with the potential for professional leadership who demonstrates academic and professional excellence, sound personal qualities, a commitment to education, demonstrated world citizenship, and committed to life-long learning

---

PROFESSIONAL PROFILE

- Dedicated, capable, and modernistic instructor striving to help students change below average grades into above average grades
- Supports colleagues and administration in assisting each child's social and academic growth by creating an atmosphere of shared respect and open communication
- Proven great listener, excellent communicator with students and parents, with a caring and sensitive approach
- Encourages socialization, sportsmanship, good character, and cooperation
- Motivator of students encouraging physical education as an enjoyable part of life for all individuals.

EDUCATION

BA in Health, Physical Education and Recreation, May 2009
Eastern University, Anywhere, California
- Minor in Secondary Education
- Health certification

SKILLS AND ACCOMPLISHMENTS

Unit Plan Development
- Developed a detailed unit plan to instruct a 75 minute class about the game of basketball.
- Used a variety of reading strategies in different lessons throughout the unit
- Integrated math into the unit while playing basketball
- Used both hands on learning and research based learning

Lesson Plan Development
- Developed many detailed lesson plans throughout the years for education classes
- Integrated different subjects into the physical education or health classes
- Used a variety of reading strategies in certain lesson plans

EXPERIENCE IN EDUCATION

Observation Hours
- Schilling Elementary, Anywhere, California, Spring 2007
- Lakewood Middle, Anywhere, California, Fall 2007
- South High, Anywhere, California, Spring 2008
- Lakewood Middle, Anywhere, California, Fall 2008

Emergency Substitute Teacher
- District 555, Anywhere, California, Fall 2008 – Spring 2009

Student Teacher
- West Elementary, Anywhere, California, Jan. 5, 2009 – Feb 5, 2009
- Central High, Anywhere, California, March 1, 2009 – May 15, 2009

ADDITIONAL EXPERIENCE

- Eastwood High Volunteer Football Coach, Fall 2006, 2007, 2008
- Eastwood Boys Basketball Summer League Coach, Summer 2007, 2008
- Eastwood Boys Coach Pitch Baseball Coach, Summer 2005

CERTIFICATES

- Ruby Payne Work Shop, MWU, Anywhere, California, Spring 2008
- Special Olympic Basketball Volunteer, Anywhere, California, Spring 2007 & 2008
- California Kids Fitness Day Volunteer, Anywhere, California, Spring 2006, 2007 & 2008
- Big Brothers/Big Sisters Bowl for Kids Sake, Anywhere, Ca, Spring 2009

Analysis of Sample Resume #1, Karl Turgen

There are a number of issues to be addressed with Mr. Turgen's resume, but the most glaring is the lack of specificity. Broad claims and generalizations are made with absolutely no substance to back them up. This makes for a lot of filler that adds nothing to his resume, thus reducing his chances of being contacted for an interview. Let's take a look at some examples:

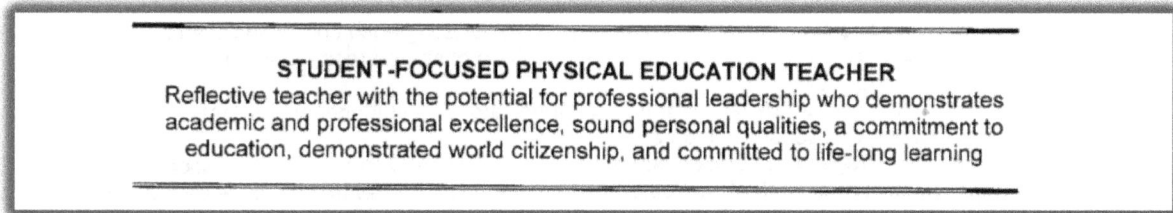

STUDENT-FOCUSED PHYSICAL EDUCATION TEACHER
Reflective teacher with the potential for professional leadership who demonstrates academic and professional excellence, sound personal qualities, a commitment to education, demonstrated world citizenship, and committed to life-long learning

---

Mr. Turgen seems to have created a personal mission statement for the opening of his resume. This isn't necessarily a terrible idea, but it didn't work well here. Let's examine what went wrong.

- "Potential for professional leadership..." What does that mean? Many people think they have the potential to be professional leaders. They could also potentially build a rocket ship and fly to Saturn, but it probably isn't going to happen.

- "Demonstrates academic and professional excellence..." Based on what? The resume indicates that Mr. Turgen has been a student teacher and a substitute teacher at this point in his life. It doesn't reveal anything that would indicate "excellence". We don't know many people who have earned the title of "academic and professional excellence." Mr. Turgen does not appear to deserve the honor yet.

- "Demonstrated world citizenship"? There is some volunteer experience cited, so maybe that is the angle he was going for, but "demonstrated world citizenship" sounds ridiculous. What does it even mean? Is it possible for someone to *not* be a world citizen? Is the applicant competing against citizens from another planet?

This section was completely unnecessary. It screams of a student who just graduated and is desperately trying to find a way to add some bulk to his resume. Resumes with inadequate information aren't good, but those with pointless filler are even worse. If we were to redo this section it would have read:

*Objective: To gain employment as a physical education teacher
and share my lifelong love of fitness with others.*

Next we encounter the "Professional Profile". This section of the resume has more of the same issues that we encountered in the mission statement. It is far too broad. Take a look:

PROFESSIONAL PROFILE

- Dedicated, capable, and modernistic instructor striving to help students change below average grades into above average grades
- Supports colleagues and administration in assisting each child's social and academic growth by creating an atmosphere of shared respect and open communication
- Proven great listener, excellent communicator with students and parents, with a caring and sensitive approach
- Encourages socialization, sportsmanship, good character, and cooperation
- Motivator of students encouraging physical education as an enjoyable part of life for all individuals.

Mr. Turgen has shared his opinion of some nice features he has to offer, but there is nothing to back up any of the statements. Are we simply supposed to take him at his word that everything listed is true? "Dedicated" and "capable"? We didn't automatically assume that the candidate was undedicated and incapable prior to receiving the resume. He hasn't done anything to prove that he is any more dedicated or capable than anyone else. "Proven great listener"? How? If there is an exam that recognizes great listeners, no one informed us. Our recommendation would be to eliminate this entire section. It serves no distinct purpose. Up next we have "Skills and Accomplishments":

SKILLS AND ACCOMPLISHMENTS

Unit Plan Development
- Developed a detailed unit plan to instruct a 75 minute class about the game of basketball.
- Used a variety of reading strategies in different lessons throughout the unit
- Integrated math into the unit while playing basketball
- Used both hands on learning and research based learning

Lesson Plan Development
- Developed many detailed lesson plans throughout the years for education classes
- Integrated different subjects into the physical education or health classes
- Used a variety of reading strategies in certain lesson plans

---

There are some good ideas here, but a resume simply isn't the place for them. There is no way that Mr. Turgen can authentically demonstrate with bullet points what he is trying to convey. If he were to take a well polished lesson plan that incorporated these ideas and pair it with a video of him carrying out the lesson, that may catch someone's eye. If it were to show up in a potential employer's mailbox as part of an electronic portfolio, they may indeed give it a watch.

"Developed many detailed lesson plans throughout the years" never should have been used. Employers can smell an exaggeration from a mile away and Mr. Turgen does not have enough experience yet to make this claim. "Experience in Education" is our next section:

Observation Hours
- Schilling Elementary, Anywhere, California, Spring 2007
- Lakewood Middle, Anywhere, California, Fall 2007
- South High, Anywhere, California, Spring 2008
- Lakewood Middle, Anywhere, California, Fall 2008

Emergency Substitute Teacher
- District 555, Anywhere, California, Fall 2008 – Spring 2009

Student Teacher
- West Elementary, Anywhere, California, Jan. 5, 2009 – Feb 5, 2009
- Central High, Anywhere, California, March 1, 2009 – May 15, 2009

This section looks fairly solid, except that there seems to be some confusion about the heading. Wasn't it supposed to be "Experience in Education?" Where did it go? If you look back at the original resume you will find it on page one, while the excerpt above is on page two. Mr. Turgen should have corrected this issue. Headings should always stay above their corresponding material. Finally we encounter the closing section of the document:

ADDITIONAL EXPERIENCE

- Eastwood High Volunteer Football Coach, Fall 2006, 2007, 2008
- Eastwood Boys Basketball Summer League Coach, Summer 2007, 2008
- Eastwood Boys Coach Pitch Baseball Coach, Summer 2005

CERTIFICATES

- Ruby Payne Work Shop, MWU, Anywhere, California, Spring 2008
- Special Olympic Basketball Volunteer, Anywhere, California, Spring 2007 & 2008
- California Kids Fitness Day Volunteer, Anywhere, California, Spring 2006, 2007 & 2008
- Big Brothers/Big Sisters Bowl for Kids Sake, Anywhere, Ca, Spring 2009

This section needs further polishing to correct typographical errors, illogical sequencing on dates and jargon use (in the form of an acronym). All three of these items are readily apparent in this extremely condensed area.

Multiple apostrophes were omitted and "Olympic" needs to be pluralized. Just because an individual applies for a physical education position does not mean that they are exempt from grammatical rules.

The dates in the certificates section seem to be listed at random. Why are they not in a logical order? The most popular style on a resume is to start with the most recent date and work backwards. The opposite can be appropriate under the correct circumstances (when it presents your experience as more relevant to the desired job), but to use no order at all is unacceptable.

Also, while not a typo, what is "MWU"? The logical guess is that it is a university, but which one is not readily apparent. We know of at least three different universities that use that acronym and none of them are in the applicant's home state of California. It's not an abbreviation for where Mr. Turgen's coursework was done, so it's not an alma mater. Why would the location of a workshop he attended be relevant? Given no explanation, it could really stand for anything. Hopefully it isn't "Marsupials Without Umbrellas". Nothing smells worse than a wet marsupial.

Mr. Turgen needs to rethink this entire resume. With some eliminations, substitutions and corrections he can transform it into a much more powerful document.

On the following page we will use our resume rubric to pinpoint both the strengths and weaknesses of Mr. Turgen's work. The rubric is broken into two separate columns, "Fail" and "Pass." Which rank this particular resume receives is specified by a gray highlight in each category.

A resume does not always have to achieve a "Pass" in every section to be successful. There is no specific number of "Pass" rankings that need to be received before the resume may be capable of acquiring an interview for the applicant. The only true determination of how polished a resume needs to be is the quality of the other resumes that it will be competing against. With that being said, why leave anything in doubt? You need to make sure that your resume is more impressive than the competition. Mr. Turgen failed in this regard.

No Educator Left Behind
Resume Rubric

	Fail	Pass
Format	Formatting (font size, font type, punctuation, capitalization, bullets, etc.) is inconsistent	Formatting (font size, font type, punctuation, capitalization, bullets, etc.) is consistent
	Not all mandatory headings (Education, Experience, References) are represented	All mandatory headings (Education, Experience, References) are represented
	White space is inadequate or excessive	White space is appropriate
Education	Education does not meet requirements	Education meets requirements
	Dates are not in a logical order	Dates are in a logical order
	Certifications are not listed	Certifications are listed
Experience	Experience does not meet requirements	Experience does meet requirements
	Dates are not in a logical order	Dates are in a logical order
	Job duties are general and/or irrelevant	Job duties are specific and relevant
Editing	Typographical and/or grammatical errors are present (confirmed by multiple editors)	No typographical and/or grammatical errors are present (confirmed by multiple editors)
	Inaccurate and/or false information	No inaccurate and/or false information
Wording	Weak and/or unprofessional vocabulary	Strong and/or professional vocabulary
	Inconsistent tenses	Consistent Tenses
	Wording is confusing and difficult to read	Wording is clear and easy to read
	An excessive amount of jargon is present	Jargon is not excessive
	Unnecessary information is present	Unnecessary information has been removed
Length	Inappropriate length (three pages or more, plus references)	Appropriate length (one or two pages plus references)
References	References are not listed	References are listed
	References are not listed in a consistent format (name, title, contact information)	References are listed consistently (name, title, contact information)
	No supervisors are listed	Supervisors are listed

Wanda A. Stine
8521 Conners ▪ Anywhere, KS 66801 ▪ 555-555-4974 ▪ wstine@email.edu

Objective
To obtain a teaching position in an elementary school

Education

East State University
BA in Elementary Education
Anticipated graduation date May 2011

West High School
High school diploma received in May 2007

Teaching Experience

Student Teacher (Intern), 8/10 to Present
Erving USD 253, Anywhere, KS
3rd grade
Teach lessons I have written and plans my mentor teacher has written, walk the students to and from specials, attend teacher in-services, and teach a math intervention group

Other Experience

Elementary Classroom Tutor
Spring Semester 2009
Tutoring kindergarten students with their alphabet and numbers three hours a week

Youth Friends
January 2007 to May 2007
Mentored students in small groups and one-on-one situations in kindergarten and first grade
Helped with math, reading, and spelling
Taught a lesson on bullying with the kindergarten class

Girl Scout Gold Award
October 2006
Planned and hosted a Halloween "fun night" for children in the community

Assistant Manager
Pizza Place, Anywhere, KS 66801
May 2005 to May 2010

Secretary
Smith's Law Office
May 2007 to June 2009

Honors
Dean's Honor List for the semesters of Spring 2008, Spring 2009, Fall 2009, and Spring 2010
Member of Kappa Delta Pi since 2009

References

Carol Neems (Mentor Teacher)
Voyage Elementary School, USD 900
3355 West 19th Ave.
Anywhere, KS 55501
555-555-2282
cneems@email.com

Dwight Hook (Student Teaching Supervisor)
East State University
1500 Educational St.
Anywhere, KS 55502
620-341-5651
dhook@email.com

Bill Romo (Pizza Place Owner)
Pizza Place
1000 Industrial Rd.
Anywhere, KS 55503
555-555-9984

Analysis of Sample Resume #2, Wanda Stine

Ms. Stine has a very common resume issue: mediocrity. There is nothing extraordinary that stands out. The aesthetics are passable, but they aren't ideal. The document has been edited to the point that there aren't egregious errors, but it lacks polishing. The wording delivers the message, but it does it in a very lackluster fashion. In a word, this resume is bland. Let's take a closer look:

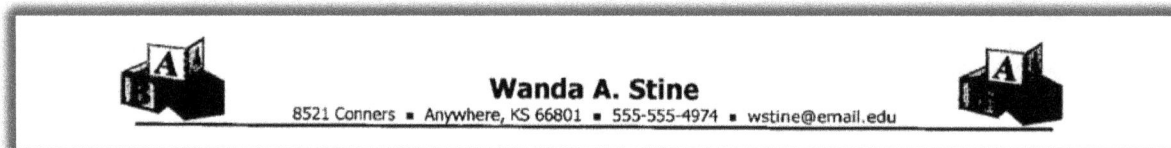

Wanda A. Stine
8521 Conners ▪ Anywhere, KS 66801 ▪ 555-555-4974 ▪ wstine@email.edu

The building blocks in the corner of this resume are probably the most noticeable portion of the entire document, but unfortunately they create issues of their own. According to Ms. Stine's objective, she is looking for an elementary position. When an applicant says "elementary position" they are typically referring to kindergarten through 5th or 6th grade. However, even if it was unintended, the building blocks on this page seem to say, "I want to teach preschool or kindergarten." There is nothing wrong with a special twist to your resume that will add some flare, but make sure it doesn't send an unintentional message.

Forget about what the resume says and focus solely on the structure. Where is the focal point? It's the blocks, right? Where should it be? The applicant's name, of course! Wanda could benefit by pumping the font size on her name up a few notches. The objective section is the next culprit:

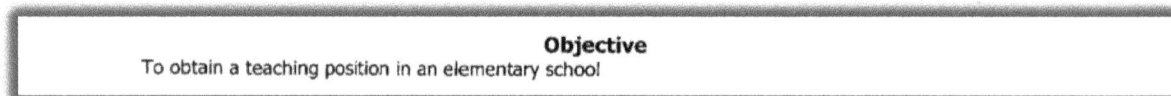

Objective
To obtain a teaching position in an elementary school

That's as straightforward and to the point as they come. We have no issues with brevity, but it might be a little _too_ brief. It's certainly better than rambling on for three or four lines about nothing. With the whole sentence veering to the left side of the page it makes for a terribly unbalanced feeling.

We can guess what the applicant was thinking: _"The rest of the resume is left aligned so I should probably stick with that theme."_ Consistency is nice, but not at the cost of presentation. If the objective is going to remain that short it should be centered. Ms. Stine also shouldn't be scared to add a couple of words that will take the edge off of the simplicity. Take a look at the result:

Objective
To obtain an elementary teaching position where I can share my love of learning.

It bears mentioning that objective statements are not even necessary if you specify your desired position within the cover letter (or if you are open to any available jobs). Education is the next item on Ms. Stine's resume:

Education

East State University
BA in Elementary Education
Anticipated graduation date May 2011

West High School
High school diploma received in May 2007

Two quick changes could be made to benefit Ms. Stine. The high school diploma needs to be eliminated. Her graduation from high school is assumed and adds nothing to improving her resume. Secondly, clarification on her teaching certificate would be helpful. If Ms. Stine already had teaching experience somewhere we could make the logical jump that her license was current. However, since Ms. Stine has yet to graduate we don't know that her certificate has been obtained. The teaching experience portion is next and there are some items that need addressed:

Teaching Experience

Student Teacher (Intern), 8/10 to Present
Erving USD 253, Anywhere, KS
3rd grade
Teach lessons I have written and plans my mentor teacher has written, walk the students to and from specials, attend teacher in-services, and teach a math intervention group

---

The first issue is an extremely quick fix and all too common in resumes. The date is listed as "8/10". That's fine, but in the rest of the resume the date is written out (August 2010). Not only that, but on the other experience entries the date comes on the line below the job (not next to it, as demonstrated in the example above). Either way is fine, but pick one method to list dates and stay with it throughout the course of the entire document. Switching back and forth will make your resume look awkward.

Secondly, why is the school not listed? Where in the district did Ms. Stine teach? Employers want to know what kind of experience applicants have, which is determined by the schools in which they have worked. School names should be listed so there is no guess work involved. This holds true even if the experience comes from a small district where there was only one school available.

The sentence that accompanies this section is in desperate need of a rewrite. Once again, it's far too average. What student teacher hasn't taken on those types of responsibilities? No employer skims through resumes thinking, *"I just have to locate someone with experience walking students from one location to another."* Some specifics would go a long way here. A revision of this section might look something like:

> *Student Teacher, Erving USD 900, Anywhere, KS (August 2010 to Present)*
> *I am working in a third grade classroom at Washington Elementary School this semester. My responsibilities include implementing a math curriculum that utilizes Everyday Math, creating lesson plans with Gagne's Events of Instruction, and differentiating instruction for groups with multiple skill levels during their tier time.*

These specifics might grab the attention of a potential employer. *"Everyday Math? We use that series too. This applicant might be able to hit the ground running."* The sentence structure in the above section isn't our favorite technique, but that's not to say that it isn't acceptable. We prefer bullet points. Given how busy people reviewing resumes are and how little time they are likely to dedicate to each resume, it seems logical to share the relevant information in as quick and concise a manner as possible. With her teaching information presented, Ms. Stine then listed "Other Experience":

Other Experience

Elementary Classroom Tutor
Spring Semester 2009
Tutoring kindergarten students with their alphabet and numbers three hours a week

Youth Friends
January 2007 to May 2007
Mentored students in small groups and one-on-one situations in kindergarten and first grade
Helped with math, reading, and spelling
Taught a lesson on bullying with the kindergarten class

Girl Scout Gold Award
October 2006
Planned and hosted a Halloween "fun night" for children in the community

Assistant Manager
Pizza Place, Anywhere, KS 66801
May 2005 to May 2010

Secretary
Smith's Law Office
May 2007 to June 2009

While there is nothing necessarily "wrong" here, once again we have a section that is about as exciting as filing your taxes. These are quality experiences, but they need a spark. Rethinking some of the wording could help considerably.

"Tutoring kindergarten students with their alphabet and numbers three hours a week" sounds awkward. It happened in the past, so why isn't it in past tense? "Tutor" was already in the job title, so why is "Tutoring" the verb? "Three hours a week" is not a quantity of time to brag about, so why include it?

A more captivating choice of words should have been used. "Reviewed alphabet and number sense skills with kindergarten students" is more appealing to the eye.

Ms. Stine closes with her references and this is easily the most well done portion of her resume:

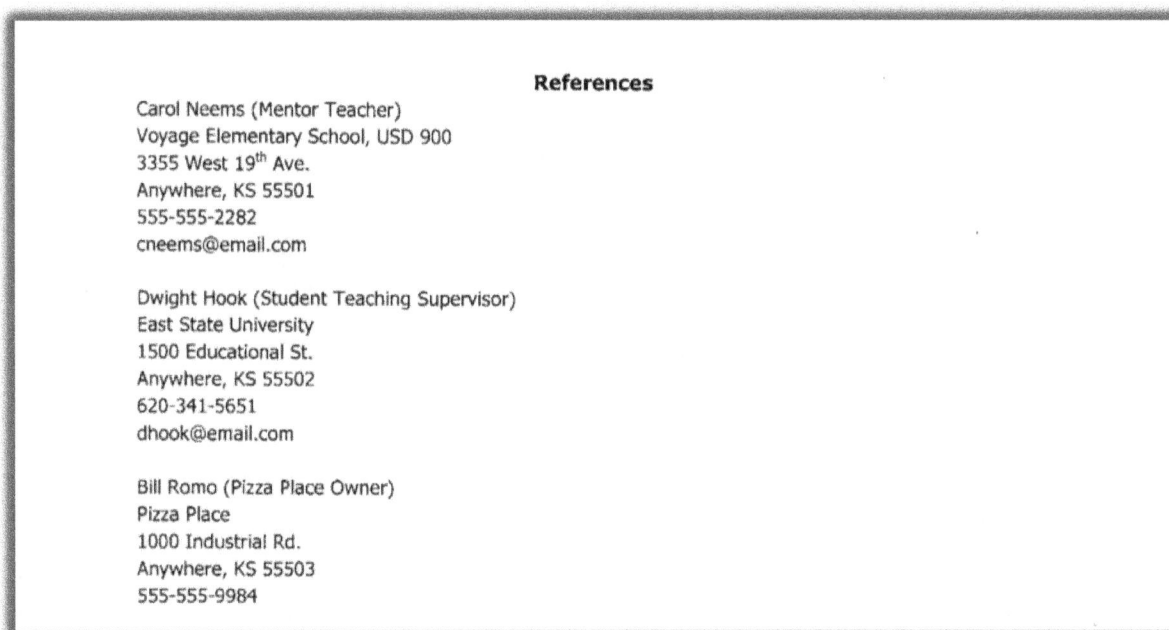

References

Carol Neems (Mentor Teacher)
Voyage Elementary School, USD 900
3355 West 19th Ave.
Anywhere, KS 55501
555-555-2282
cneems@email.com

Dwight Hook (Student Teaching Supervisor)
East State University
1500 Educational St.
Anywhere, KS 55502
620-341-5651
dhook@email.com

Bill Romo (Pizza Place Owner)
Pizza Place
1000 Industrial Rd.
Anywhere, KS 55503
555-555-9984

The format looks great, the information is easy to read and there are multiple ways to contact each reference (an email would have been nice for the third one, but it isn't always an option). Most importantly, all three references are former or current supervisors. Prospective employers want to be able to discuss performance with previous bosses. Give them what they want.

Ms. Stine's resume is by no means a lost cause. With the minor changes listed above it can become a quality resume. It isn't ready to be submitted yet, but it's close. The following page shows how we scored Ms. Stine's resume with the aid of our Resume Rubric.

No Educator Left Behind
Resume Rubric

	Fail	Pass
Format	Formatting (font size, font type, punctuation, capitalization, bullets, etc.) is inconsistent	Formatting (font size, font type, punctuation, capitalization, bullets, etc.) is consistent
	Not all mandatory headings (Education, Experience, References) are represented	All mandatory headings (Education, Experience, References) are represented
	White space is inadequate or excessive	White space is appropriate
Education	Education does not meet requirements	Education meets requirements
	Dates are not in a logical order	Dates are in a logical order
	Certifications are not listed	Certifications are listed
Experience	Experience does not meet requirements	Experience does meet requirements
	Dates are not in a logical order	Dates are in a logical order
	Job duties are general and/or irrelevant	Job duties are specific and relevant
Editing	Typographical and/or grammatical errors are present (confirmed by multiple editors)	No typographical and/or grammatical errors are present (confirmed by multiple editors)
	Inaccurate and/or false information	No inaccurate and/or false information
Wording	Weak and/or unprofessional vocabulary	Strong and/or professional vocabulary
	Inconsistent tenses	Consistent Tenses
	Wording is confusing and difficult to read	Wording is clear and easy to read
	An excessive amount of jargon is present	Jargon is not excessive
	Unnecessary information is present	Unnecessary information has been removed
Length	Inappropriate length (three pages or more, plus references)	Appropriate length (one or two pages plus references)
References	References are not listed	References are listed
	References are not listed in a consistent format (name, title, contact information)	References are listed consistently (name, title, contact information)
	No supervisors are listed	Supervisors are listed

Denise D. Williams

1178 25th Ave.
Anywhere, CO 55552
(555) 555-421
dwilliams@email.edu

OBJECTIVE

I will help children realize their potential and foster a love for science in a student-centered environment by thoughtfully teaching curriculum and skills that cultivate life long learning.

EDUCATION

Jefferson State University, Anywhere, Colorado
Bachelor's of Science degree in Secondary Education. 3.34 grade point average on a 4.0 scale. Graduated, December 2010.

Jefferson State University, Anywhere, Colorado
Bachelor's of Science degree in Biology and a Minor in Chemistry. 3.29 grade point average on a 4.0 scale. Graduated, May 2010.

EXPERIENCE

Student Teacher, North High School, Anywhere, Colorado
Biology and Chemistry
September 2010 – December 2010
Primarily taught sophomore and junior level biology and chemistry with self-created lesson plans that integrate Colorado State Science Standards with technology and emphasis towards student-centeredness.

Student Observer and Aide, Roosevelt High School, Anywhere, Colorado
Anatomy and Earth Science
February 2010- May 2010
Assisted students with identifying the location and name of human body parts through self-created lessons. Helped students identify minerals by looking at the specific characteristics they possess, and also supervised students during dissections.

Student Observer, Cunningham High School, Anywhere, Colorado
Biology, Physical Science, and Chemistry
March 2009-April 2009
Observed students learning a variety of subjects including mitosis, metric conversions, and chemical reactions.

Substitute, Developmental Services of Southwest Colorado.
May 2007-August 2007, May 2008-August 2008
Led and supervised daily educational and life programs for young adults and senior citizens who had developmental disabilities. The programs included morning exercises, daily hygiene etiquette, communication skills, and basic curriculum such as art, culture, English, math and science.

Biology Tutor, Kelly Center at Jefferson State University.
April 2007-May 2010
Assisted students with their homework and questions.

**HONORS/
ACTIVITIES**

- President of Student Alumni Association, fall 2007-spring 2008.
- JSU Cross Country and Track team member, summer 2006-spring 2007.
- Shadowed live surgical procedures under the supervision of Dr. Bret Grizzell, summer 2008.
- Officiated MAYB (basketball) and other summer basketball leagues, spring 2007-summer 2008.
- Vice President of the Biology Club, fall 2006-spring 2007.
- Volunteer for the elderly at Horizons Hospital, spring 2008-summer 2008.
- Volleyball women's league champion, JSU intramural volleyball, fall 2009.
- Team captain of the JSU intramural basketball champions, spring 2009.
- Experienced farmer (working knowledge of livestock, agriculture, etc.)

**Sample Resume #3, Denise Williams (page two)**

REFERENCES   **Jerry Donovan**
USD 555 Superintendent
900 North Mission Street
Anywhere, CO 55541
(555) 555-2939

Bill White
Principal, North High School
1500 Washington Avenue
Anywhere, CO 55541
(555) 555-8900

Nina Martinez
North High School Biology Teacher
1500 Washington Avenue
Anywhere, CO 55524
(555) 555-4620

Analysis of Sample Resume #3, Denise Williams

This resume was well thought out and stands a solid chance of landing an interview with a prospective employer. Let's take a closer look at some of the individual sections starting with "Education".

EDUCATION	**Jefferson State University, Anywhere, Colorado** Bachelor's of Science degree in Secondary Education. 3.34 grade point average on a 4.0 scale. Graduated, December 2010.
	Jefferson State University, Anywhere, Colorado Bachelor's of Science degree in Biology and a Minor in Chemistry. 3.29 grade point average on a 4.0 scale. Graduated, May 2010.

Sometimes aspiring teachers have put in extra work and obtained a higher level of education than what is necessary. Ms. Williams has completed two bachelor's degrees, which only makes her more desirable to employers. Applicants should be sure to list any certificates, licenses, or degrees they have earned in addition to their bachelor's degree. We are guessing that Ms. Williams probably has her teaching certificate at this point, but because she is a recent graduate with no experience, it can't be assumed. It would benefit her to mention this.

The only other modification that we would suggest in this section would be to eliminate the words "grade point average on a 4.0 scale." It's unnecessary. If Jefferson State uses an insane variation of typical grades, like a 7.0 scale, then an explanation may be warranted. Everyone is going to assume that the scale is the standard four point variety, so there is no need to list that information. "3.34 GPA" would have sufficed.

One could also argue that there is no point to include GPAs. This is typically true. However, for aspiring teachers who are fresh out of college, a 4.0 (or similarly high) GPA may give them an edge. There is no need for applicants who have already obtained teaching experience to list their GPAs. Let's move on to "Experience":

EXPERIENCE	**Student Teacher, North High School, Anywhere, Colorado** Biology and Chemistry September 2010 – December 2010 Primarily taught sophomore and junior level biology and chemistry with self-created lesson plans that integrate Colorado State Science Standards with technology and emphasis towards student-centeredness.
	Student Observer and Aide, Roosevelt High School, Anywhere, Colorado Anatomy and Earth Science February 2010- May 2010 Assisted students with identifying the location and name of human body parts through self-created lessons. Helped students identify minerals by looking at the specific characteristics they possess, and also supervised students during dissections.

Typically we recommend bullet points for job descriptions, but narrative form seems to work well here. Don't be afraid to try multiple styles when constructing your resume. You'll know the winner when you see it. The next section is "Honors/Activities":

HONORS/ ACTIVITIES	- President of Student Alumni Association, fall 2007-spring 2008. - JSU Cross Country and Track team member, summer 2006-spring 2007. - Shadowed live surgical procedures under the supervision of Dr. Bret Grizzell, summer 2008. - Officiated MAYB (basketball) and other summer basketball leagues, spring 2007-summer 2008. - Vice President of the Biology Club, fall 2006-spring 2007. - Volunteer for the elderly at Horizons Hospital, spring 2008-summer 2008. - Volleyball women's league champion, JSU intramural volleyball, fall 2009. - Team captain of the JSU intramural basketball champions, spring 2009. - Experienced farmer (working knowledge of livestock, agriculture, etc.)

A nice collection of experiences and they're all relevant. There are a collection of items that relate to science, leadership and athletics. We're assuming that Ms. Williams intends to get involved with sports at her new place of employment. Having the knowledge and being willing to coach/sponsor athletics and activities makes an applicant more employable. The only issue here is that the items should have been organized by date. While this is more important in the "Education" and "Experience" sections, it still should have been done here as well. The resume concludes with "References".

REFERENCES	**Jerry Donovan** USD 555 Superintendent 900 North Mission Street Anywhere, CO 55541 (555) 555-2939 **Bill White** Principal, North High School 1500 Washington Avenue Anywhere, CO 55541 (555) 555-8900 **Nina Martinez** North High School Biology Teacher 1500 Washington Avenue Anywhere, CO 55524 (555) 555-4620

There are no issues here. Two of the references are supervisors and one is a teacher at a school where Ms. Williams taught. Some experts advise that putting the same header from the front of your resume on your reference page is a necessity. Ms. Williams didn't do this and we don't take issue with it. Adding your name and contact information to the reference page is a nice touch, but it isn't a deal breaker.

We're organized enough to keep the two pages together and don't have any problem with glancing back at the first page if we need to review the contact information.

This is a solid resume for a new teacher and is likely to provide Ms. Williams with opportunities to interview. Let's further examine this document with the assistance of our Resume Rubric.

No Educator Left Behind
Resume Rubric

	Fail	Pass
Format	Formatting (font size, font type, punctuation, capitalization, bullets, etc.) is inconsistent	Formatting (font size, font type, punctuation, capitalization, bullets, etc.) is consistent
	Not all mandatory headings (Education, Experience, References) are represented	All mandatory headings (Education, Experience, References) are represented
	White space is inadequate or excessive	White space is appropriate
Education	Education does not meet requirements	Education meets requirements
	Dates are not in a logical order	Dates are in a logical order
	Certifications are not listed	Certifications are listed
Experience	Experience does not meet requirements	Experience does meet requirements
	Dates are not in a logical order	Dates are in a logical order
	Job duties are general and/or irrelevant	Job duties are specific and relevant
Editing	Typographical and/or grammatical errors are present (confirmed by multiple editors)	No typographical and/or grammatical errors are present (confirmed by multiple editors)
	Inaccurate and/or false information	No inaccurate and/or false information
Wording	Weak and/or unprofessional vocabulary	Strong and/or professional vocabulary
	Inconsistent tenses	Consistent Tenses
	Wording is confusing and difficult to read	Wording is clear and easy to read
	An excessive amount of jargon is present	Jargon is not excessive
	Unnecessary information is present	Unnecessary information has been removed
Length	Inappropriate length (three pages or more, plus references)	Appropriate length (one or two pages plus references)
References	References are not listed	References are listed
	References are not listed in a consistent format (name, title, contact information)	References are listed consistently (name, title, contact information)
	No supervisors are listed	Supervisors are listed

Applications

"The closest to perfection that a person ever comes is when he fills out a job application form."
~ Stanley J. Randall

Applications can add an interesting wrinkle to the process of finding a job. When applying to individual districts, some will require them, while some won't. Educational applications can often be frustrating. If you've filled many of them out, you have probably experienced this. The questions can be repetitive, obscure, and even pointless.

Recently one of our teachers was going through this process. She was extremely stressed because the application asked how many credit hours she had accumulated to obtain her minor in psychology. She had been pouring over her transcript and university documents trying to determine which courses counted and which courses should be credited towards her major. A number of the courses seemed like they could be applied towards both which was further muddying the waters. Rather than help her find the true answer to the question, it was time to share a dirty little secret of the application process. *No one is verifying your answer on those types of questions.* Rest assured that in 99% of school districts there is no one who has the time to check that you added up your credits for a minor correctly.

We're not telling you to lie, but it is okay to give an answer that is in the ballpark and not stress. You will not improve or lessen your chances of obtaining the job based on giving a precise answer to a question that no one will verify. Now, if you give a bizarre answer that arouses suspicion or inaccurate information that a potential employer would know is false, you're going to create problems for yourself. Honestly though, is anyone going to verify your high school GPA? Nope. Is anyone going to do the research to see whether your answer of 3.5 is correct? Unlikely. Get as close to the right answer as possible without undo amounts of stress and then move on with your life. If you can't find the answer to obscure questions, then estimate. It does not matter whether you made $7.00 or $7.50 per hour at your part time job prior to graduating. If you can't remember the exact pay then pick one and move on.

What is truly examined on an application? Qualifications, experience, references and responses to short answer questions. If you sound foolish or have typos, you're out of contention. End of story. Just like with your resume, have someone who will give you honest feedback proofread your applications. Copy and paste your responses into an email and send them to someone if you don't have a trusted proofreader on hand. Don't cost yourself an opportunity over something careless.

Another source of stress that has thankfully become much less common in recent years are applications that are not compatible with word processors (you can't enter your personal information with the use of a computer). Hopefully you don't run into one of these antiques, but if you should there are three ways to handle it:

- Use immaculate handwriting. If you've got it, here is your opportunity to flaunt it. Some people would never recommend this idea to you as they claim it would look unprofessional. We're tempted to recommend that you not consider working for a district that would put you in this predicament to begin with, but in keeping an open mind we'll just tell you that outstanding penmanship is acceptable.

- Find someone who has a typewriter and see if they can help you. For those that are young enough that you don't know what a typewriter is, it's like a computer that can't log on to Facebook. Pretty lame, huh?

- If you have a decent level of tech savvy then use a workaround to enter text into the application anyway. There are a number of ways to manage this (depending on with what type of document you are dealing).

To help lower the amount of anxiety that accompanies applications, it would serve you well to keep any information you may need repeatedly readily available. It is extremely frustrating to search at length for obscure information only to have to do it again when a future application asks the same question. If you print a copy of every application that you complete (or store each one electronically) then you can save yourself undo stress in the future. Other items to have on hand are:

- Education: Enrollment and graduation dates, names of degrees, total number of credit hours, credits acquired for minors and concentrations, GPAs, awards, honors and transcripts are all useful to have available.

- Experience: The name of a previous workplace is likely easy enough to remember, but addresses, contact information for supervisors, dates of employment and salaries can be a bit trickier.

- Certificates: The types, expiration and any specific numbers on the certificate can all come in handy. If you make a copy of your certificate(s) to refer to it will help.

- Activities: Many applications will ask what types of activities you are willing to sponsor or coach. If your list is short, then this isn't an issue. However, if you have a longer list and keep it with the rest of your information then you will not have to start from scratch on each application.

- Responses To Common Questions: Many applications have short response sections. Often they have the same (or versions of the same) questions. If you save copies of your responses then you will not have to recreate them each time. Common examples of these questions are:
  - What is your philosophy of education?
  - Why are you applying to our district?
  - What additional information would you like to share with us?

There is one other item that will be on nearly any application that you fill out; a question asking if you have ever been convicted of a felony. There is no way around this one. If you are a district's desired candidate then they will do a background check prior to hiring you, so honesty is your best policy. If you have any activities in your life that could lead to felony charges, make it your priority to clean them up now. Then, when you're ready, come in a true pursuit of an educational job.

Chapter Five: Resumes And Applications
Applying For A Job In A Different State

"The doors we open and close each day decide the lives we live."
~ Flora Whittemore

Each year, many people apply for out of state positions. A large percentage of those applicants will not be considered. Why?

Every state has its own set of criteria to determine who is qualified to work in the field of education. Employers have to take this into consideration when deciding if an out-of-state applicant will have the proper certification to work in their school.

If you are applying for an out-of-state job that you are serious about, you need to take a few steps to become a realistic contender.

- Determine what is required to become certified in the state to which you are applying. Then determine what will be necessary for you to do to meet those requirements.

- Let the human resources department (or whomever is responsible for hiring) know that you are aware of the requirements in their district/state and that you are working towards them. Fifteen years of experience in a bordering state does not necessarily qualify you for the position. If you are serious about moving to a new location, get your ducks in a row and start working towards the appropriate credentials.

- Be certain that you state in your cover letter that you are working towards fulfilling all of the state's requirements for certification. It would also be wise to discuss your rationale for the move. If someone wants to make a radical geographical change, it often leaves a potential employer curious as to why.

Personal contact cannot be stressed enough in this situation. Out of state applications can be questionable to those doing the hiring, so clarifying your intentions with an employer can go a long way towards improving your odds.

One final note for those of you that are considering a job in another state; please do your homework on the cost of living in the area to which you are applying. If you see that one area is paying their teachers ten to twenty thousand dollars more per year than what is typical, don't get too excited. Do you think that this bump in pay is just out of the goodness of their heart? Unlikely. Even though money looks the same, it spends differently all over our country. Fifty thousand dollars a year goes a whole lot further in rural Kansas then it does in Los Angeles, California.

Electronic Screening

*"Computers make it easier to do a lot of things, but most of the
things they make it easier to do don't need to be done."*
~ Andy Rooney

A practice that has become much more common in recent years is the use of an electronic screener to rate candidates who apply for educational positions. This is essentially a quiz that attempts to decide if you are a "good" candidate for the job or not. There have been numerous studies done to determine if this is an effective way to determine the quality of applicants and the results have been mixed. Whether it does a sufficient job of that task or not is beside the point; if a district requires one of these quizzes then you are stuck taking it if you apply. It has been estimated that approximately 15% of school districts across the United States are currently requiring some form of this electronic screening.[4]

After completing the quiz your results will be submitted to those that are involved in the hiring process. There is usually a cut score that has been established and individuals who score at a certain mark or higher are considered to be applicants that are worthy of an interview, while those that fail to meet the mark will not be interviewed unless there is an exception (experience or connections that would allow a candidate to be considered regardless of a poor score).

Since there is so much riding on this quiz, it obviously is in your best interest to score well upon it. So what are the correct answers? Unfortunately, there is no way to determine exactly what they are since the questions tend to be quite subjective. If you have ever taken a personality test, you will find the process very similar, except it will be from an educational standpoint. The questions are most commonly in multiple-choice format and dependent upon the district there may be short answer responses as well. An example of one possible question would be:

How do you handle challenges?

a) I work hard to solve them quickly and rationally.

b) I find someone to help me.

c) I become stressed.

d) I take my time and make sure that I overcome them.

e) I find a quiet spot and sob uncontrollably until they pass.

What is the best response to this question? It's hard to say since several seem reasonable. We can safely eliminate C and E; even if those are true for you, they probably won't score you many points. A, B, and D all have potential positives and negatives, so you would be best to answer with whatever is the most likely for you.

The responses that result in the highest scores are kept confidential, so you have to rely on your best judgment when working through an electronic screener. When considering your answers, know that the best results are achieved by those that demonstrate high levels of competence in:

- Dedication: Show your absolute commitment to the field, your prospective school, education in general, and especially to the students. These screeners frequently look for people who view teaching not as a job, but a calling.

- Differentiation: Make it apparent that you realize students have a wide variety of needs and they can all learn if given appropriate instruction.

- Relationships: Higher marks will be received by those that are comfortable building connections with students, parents, and fellow staff members. It is important to show that your realize the importance of developing and maintaining these relationships.

- Proactive Ability: Answer questions so it is obvious that you solve problems before they occur. Make it apparent that when issues do arise, you work to make sure they won't repeat themselves.

- Student Centeredness: Demonstrate that students are your number one priority. You will help them to constantly improve and put them first in all decisions, while keeping a well-maintained classroom at the same time.

There are several different types of electronic screeners available, but all have the same goal: to narrow down the candidates so only higher quality applicants remain. Your goal is to beat the screener. It's similar to a video game in nature when you think about it. Score high enough and you win. Anything else results in a "Game Over". So how can you increase your chances?

- Answer From The Heart: Don't try to out think the screener. Many of the questions will seem repetitive. This is intentional. Employers want to see if your thoughts and opinions vary. If they do, it's typically a sign that you have either been dishonest or are confused on what you believe.

- Use A Reliable Connection: This is not the time to lose your Internet connection. If you have any doubts about it then select a different location.

- Eliminate Distractions: Electronic screeners frequently have time limits, so make sure that you are in a quiet environment where you can think soundly. Screaming children, ringing cell phones and blaring televisions are not the best stimulators for rational thought.

The good news is that it doesn't take much additional work to complete a screener. There is very little prep work that can be done. Remember these tests are also not worth stressing over, because as mentioned at the beginning of this section, you will only encounter them at approximately 15% of the districts nationwide. Do your best and be yourself; that is all that can be asked of you!

"A winning effort begins with preparation."
~ Joe Gibbs

Would you like to know what an administrator thinks when they see you walk into an interview with a giant portfolio?

"Hmmmmm... I wonder how much of that I'll have to pretend to read out of common courtesy?"

There are exceptions, but the bulk of employers who are willing to be honest will tell you that they do not care about your portfolio. Mostly they view them as an assignment that you were likely required to put together for a university class prior to graduating. They may contain a well thought out "Philosophy of Education" or "Philosophy of Classroom Management" but how is one to know that those are the applicant's beliefs and not just what they thought was the "right" thing to say?

Please don't bring your portfolio to an interview and expect that employers are going to want to examine it in its entirety. If you have one or two powerful documents to share, such as impressive data you have collected, then show that specific piece to them. Maybe you have some photos that will be helpful when answering certain questions. For example, a visual with students working together while you facilitate could be a nice reference when answering a question about cooperative work. Or maybe you want to bring along a couple of well polished lesson plans so you can share them if asked about your planning.

One option is to make a copy of the portfolio for the interviewers. Then you can leave the document behind in case they would care to look over the contents later. During the interview the employers want to focus on you, not a binder. After all, you can't teach students with a portfolio, can you?

There is a twist on conventional portfolios that can make them far more productive for you. In the correct format they can be sent in advance (along with your resume, cover letter, etc) and have a far bigger impact. This can be done by the use of a DVD or website.

What if you don't have the tech savvy for this option? You probably know someone who does, right? Call in a favor. You want the finished product to look great so leave it to a professional.

The contents of the DVD/website should include your basic documents or information that you would submit to an employer (resume, cover letter, certificates). This way, if your credentials get misplaced they are still readily available to those doing the hiring. However, the most important items to include are those that will set you apart from the rest of the applicants. Some options are:

- Videos Of Lessons: One or more sample lessons could be very intriguing to employers (assuming that they are well done). Make sure to show some exciting and thought provoking material (it's not the time to show students doing worksheets).

- Photo Slideshows: When done correctly these can be extremely powerful. Quality images set to music can have a very profound effect on the viewer. Make sure that the pictures focus on your interaction with students.

- Testimonials: Video (or written references) from coworkers and/or students explaining what kind of person you are can be a nice touch.

- Lesson Plans: Are you capable of crafting a well thought out lesson? Evidence of such would be appropriate.

One word of caution: do not make any pictures/video available through a website unless you have the specific permission of those that have been included. This would be a huge breach of privacy (especially when minors are involved), so cover your bases before acting. It would even be wise to include a statement on the website stating that all participants have agreed to publically share their image.

The next step will be to distribute your DVD or invite employers to view your website. The website address can be submitted in your cover letter and/or in the body of the email when submitting all of your materials. The DVD can be mailed along with the hard copy of your credentials. Administrators frequently receive resumes and cover letters. They are the norm and often blend in with one another. If you can show your uniqueness through the aid of technology, then you will immediately be more memorable than the competition.

Are any of these items a necessity? Absolutely not. We hire people without portfolios all the time. As mentioned at the beginning of this chapter, we typically don't like seeing them because most candidates don't know how to use them correctly. Instead of referencing them for assistance in answering questions they will try to have you examine the entire binder. But for those that utilize portfolios correctly, whether hardcopy or electronic, they can be a unique tool to set an applicant apart from the crowd.

"A place for everything, everything in its place."
~ Benjamin Franklin

A number of items are often needed to complete all the steps towards applying for a job. Which documents are frequently required (or desired) by school districts?

- Cover Letter

- Resume (with References)

- District Application

- Letters of Recommendation

- Teaching License

- Transcript(s)

Our recommendation is to get the materials together and send them all at once, both electronically and as a hard copy. Why?

- It shows that you are seriously interested in the position.

- Documents (both electronic and hard copy) don't always get where they are supposed to go. Consider the second copy "insurance". If both versions arrive in the correct hands then whoever does the hiring will see your name twice. Doubling your opportunities to be noticed is certainly not a bad thing.

- Hard copies are more tangible and aesthetically pleasing than their electronic counterparts. Resume paper is heavier and has a more professional appearance than a standard sheet of copy paper.

- The person on the receiving end of the documents is not your secretary. If you send the documents over the course of five separate emails then they have to keep everything organized for you. Always strive to avoid creating extra work for others, especially when attempting to make a positive first impression.

- One item to note is that your electronic documents should be sent as PDF files. All employers should easily be able view a PDF and your formatting will be locked in. When saving your files you are able to select a number of different formats (PDF should be among them).

These documents may not be required for every position. However sending them won't hurt. Submitting your teaching license when it was not specifically asked for will not negatively impact your chances of an interview. If nothing else it shows that you are well prepared and serious about obtaining a job. But what if you don't have your license yet because you are a recent (or soon to be) graduate? This is a common occurrence. Simply explain the situation in your cover letter so there is no confusion (and no reason to exclude you from the pool of candidates).

Have a packet ready to send at a moment's notice. If you scramble to gather documents each time, it is likely that someone more organized will have their name seen first. If your materials are ready to go, you can make any necessary modifications (addresses, names, specific rationale for why you are a good fit for the job, etc.) and send the forms on their way. Your teaching license and transcripts can be kept in bulk since they require no modifications. Everything else requires some consideration and modification to give it a personal touch. This may even be true for your letters of recommendation; depending on the position, you may want people who can better discuss what makes you qualified for that particular position. Promptness is important, but not at the expense of quality.

Why is being prompt desirable? If there are multiple applicants, being the first one makes you immediately noticeable. If your packet arrives at the same time as the rest of the candidates then it will have to duel with the competition. If you apply after the application window has closed, then your chances of landing the job have likely closed as well.

Keeping a simple list of where you have applied will help keep you organized. Once you complete the necessary requirements and send off all the requested documentation, add the location and date to your list of completed submissions. It may seem like it wouldn't be an issue, but if you apply to a large number of districts simultaneously it can sometimes become confusing.

Many aspiring teachers who are approaching graduation, or have recently graduated, enlist the help of a university placement office to assist with submitting documents. Numerous colleges have this service and they can keep all of your credentials on hand. When asked, they will send all the materials to your desired location. They can also provide advice to many of your job search questions. Often these services are included as a part of a student's tuition fees, so their use comes at no additional cost.

Once all the proper documents are submitted, what many consider to be the most difficult portion of the process begins; waiting. Patience is a must, but the wait to hear (or not hear) from the districts where you have applied can be agonizing. Many applicants become curious if they should call and check to see where the employers are in the process. A word of advice on this front; don't annoy people if you want to have any shot of being hired. What you can do is make a phone call to the human resources department and touch base with whomever is available after you have submitted your documents. It should sound similar to:

"Hi, my name is Mr. X and I recently submitted my application and other documents for the English opening that you have posted. I wanted to confirm that you have received everything you need. I was also curious if a timeline has been set for interviews."

Then continue to be patient and wait to see what happens. Maybe things will go in your favor, maybe they won't. Resist the urge to continue calling back. What shall you do to pass the time while waiting patiently? Continue your job search! Keep a close watch on openings as they become available and continue to apply. Every position that you attempt to obtain increases your odds of being hired. Stay vigilant!

Chapter Five: Resumes and Applications

Activities and Discussion

Welcome to the activities and discussion section for chapter five. Everything you need to participate is located on the website that accompanies this book:

www.nelb.info

- Watch as we create a resume from start to finish in the Chapter Five Forum under "Resume Tutorial".

- Post your resume in the Chapter Five Forum in the thread "Resumes". Give constructive feedback to at least one other user who has posted a resume. You may use the resume rubric to help guide your critique. Remember to put yourself in the shoes of an employer. If you only had a moment to look over the resume, what would you see?

- Try your resume in a different format. If you are using bullets, try a narrative approach with complete sentences. If you have your resume structured horizontally, try using columns. There are many different options. Compare the new resume with your original. Which do you like better and why? Share your thoughts in the Chapter Five Forum in the thread "Resume Styles".

- Find examples of our electronic portfolios by visiting the thread in the Chapter Five Forum called "Electronic Portfolios". If you create your own, please submit the link in this thread so others may view your work.

- There are an abundance of frustrating and ridiculous questions on applications. Share the worst that you come across in the Chapter Five Forum under "Application Atrocities".

* In addition to your own thoughts, you are welcome to respond to the posts of other users. Please make sure to protect the private information of others at all times on our website. Use pseudonyms and eliminate any contact information for individuals referenced. Thank you for your cooperation.

Chapter Six

Phone Etiquette

Great Blunders In Job Search History

Moments after inventing the telephone, Mr. Bell is harassed by telemarketers, bombarded with calls from his mother-in-law and completely caught off guard by a request for an interview.

Opening Story

Recently our school had an opening and one resume in particular caught my eye. The gentleman was well qualified, the resume was solid and the experience was just what I had in mind. I called immediately to set up an interview.

The candidate answered and after the customary greetings I asked if there would be a good time for him to come and visit us. He responded with, "Well, your school is almost two hundred miles away. Can we do a phone interview instead? It's a long way out there and if I don't get the job I don't want to waste my time."

At that point my decision was already made. "I don't want to waste your time either sir. If you can't make the effort to drive here then I think I've got my answer. Have a good day and good luck with your job search."

Applying for jobs if you aren't interested or committed to the prospect is a waste of *everyone's* time, not just yours. There are things in life that you can do without making them a priority; finding a job is not one of them.

~ Beth, Principal

When An Interview Is Offered

"The bathtub was invented in 1850 and the telephone in 1875. In other words, if you had been living in 1850, you could have sat in the bathtub for 25 years without having to answer the phone."
~ Bill DeWitt

Congratulations. Your resume did the job and you have been contacted for an interview. Keep the phone call short, sweet and extremely respectful.

You are encouraged to show gratitude and enthusiasm for the opportunity. We've called people to set up an interview and they have responded as if we were the dentist confirming an appointment. Although unintended, this apathetic reply raises a number of questions about the candidate before the interview even begins.

When the employer asks if you are available to come in for an interview on a certain day or time, respond in the affirmative unless it absolutely will not work. Adjust your schedule to accommodate the interview. If you have a large enough conflict that an interview is impossible at the suggested time, then give the employer a window of times that you are available. Let them pick the day and time; that's their job, not yours.

Listen to what the caller has to say and take notes so you can remember any information that is given. Avoid asking simple questions that you can easily answer with a little research (a solid rule of thumb for life in general) such as, "Where is the school located?" You have access to the Internet and can easily find the address. If you need clarification on where the interview is held, keep it brief and professional. *"Just to confirm, I should come to the school and go to the main office, correct?"*

There are only two questions that we would recommend asking:

- *"Is there anything you would like for me to bring?"* Not only does this show your willingness to arrive prepared, but if there are still any documents needed, the employer has an opportunity to relay that information to you.

- *"May I inquire who will be interviewing me?"* This will give you a feel for what to expect. With this knowledge you can memorize individuals' names (as well as how to pronounce them) and titles prior to the interview, allowing you to focus on more pressing matters.

Most importantly, remember what your mother taught you. Be polite. *"Thank you for this opportunity, I'm looking forward to meeting you."*

Activities and Discussion

Welcome to the activities and discussion section for chapter six. Everything you need to participate is located on the website that accompanies this book:

www.nelb.info

- Watch the mock phone conversation examples that are available in the Chapter Six Forum by clicking on "Phone Conversations". Share any thoughts you have regarding the examples.

* In addition to your own thoughts, you are welcome to respond to the posts of other users. Please make sure to protect the private information of others at all times on our website. Use pseudonyms and eliminate any contact information for individuals referenced. Thank you for your cooperation.

Chapter Seven

Interview Preparation

Great Blunders In Job Search History

Fidel makes a critical error in selecting his
interview attire.

Opening Story

Do you know how I prepare for an interview? I get my "stories" ready. I have a full stable of experiences that are applicable to many of the questions that employers will likely ask and I have them all fine tuned to the point that they roll off my tongue effortlessly. One of my ready-made gems that I have used when answering questions about difficult students, parent communication, or a variety of other topics goes like this:

"During my first year of teaching, when I was instructing second grade, I had a student by the name of Scott. He was an incredibly challenging student due to his behavior and this was only amplified by my lack of experience. One day Scott had a reasonably good day; not a good day for any other student in the class, mind you, but a reasonably good day for Scott.

After school, I picked up the phone and called Scott's house to inform his parents of the news. No one picked up the phone. This was not a surprise. No one at Scott's house ever picked up the phone. His parents knew from the caller ID that the school had more bad news to share. The voicemail picked up and I left a simple message saying, "Hi, this is Scott's teacher over at the school. I just wanted to let you know that your son had a great day today! He was on task, working hard, and was very helpful. I'm looking forward to seeing him tomorrow!" I thought nothing else of this phone call and went on about my business. The next day I was sitting in the lounge eating lunch with some colleagues when a figure appeared at the door. It was Scott's mother. She was holding a pan of homemade brownies and crying. I went to her. She handed me the brownies and said, "Thank you. No one has ever told me anything good about my son before." That is the moment when I realized the power of positive communication, and in particular, positive phone calls home. No one - NO ONE - deserves to go years without hearing a kind word about their child."

I tell this story every time I interview for a position in the field of education (except in my first district where I met Scott). At this point I can tell this piece with such conviction that I have literally brought people to tears during interviews. What stories do you have that are worthy of sharing? Who is your Scott?

~ Lucas, Principal

Chapter Seven: Interview Preparation

Getting To Know Your Prospective School

"Research is to see what everybody else has seen,
and to think what nobody else has thought."
~ Albert Szent-Gyorgyi

It is amazing how many people arrive at an interview with absolutely no clue about what they are walking into. If the interviewer inquires, "What do you already know about our school?" how will you respond? This is a favorite question of employers to determine who has done their homework. Far too often the answer is, "Not much."

The real reason to be equipped with working knowledge of your potential workplace is not just to be ready for that question, but for all the others. If a question about reading is asked, you'll be at an advantage if you are familiar with the schools reading scores during recent assessments. If the interviewers ask about discipline you can work in what you've learned about the school's policies. The examples are endless and there's no excuse in this day and age to not know your prospective school prior to the interview. But where does one acquire this information?

Read over the school and district's website before arriving and check the state's website to retrieve test data. Ask the school secretary if newsletters, handbooks or other documents are available. The school handbook is of particular importance because it can give you an inside look into the school's rules, policies, and expectations. Search the Internet for news stories related to the school and district. Make sure to determine where the school is located and how long it will take you to arrive there. Arriving late for you interview does not make a good impression. Plan out when you will need to leave so that you arrive approximately ten to fifteen minutes early. It shows promptness, but won't leave you sitting and waiting for so long that it becomes awkward.

Not only is it important to do your homework on the school/district where you are interviewing, you should also research the surrounding area/city. We have found this to be especially true in smaller settings where the school is the hub of the entire community. Knowledge of the surroundings can be obtained through a number of avenues, including:

- Visiting the Community: If you have spent little or no time in the area, then take a road trip and get a feel for it. Take a stroll through town, find a spot to eat, talk to those that are open to conversation and drive around to take in the sights. Consider it your own personal field trip!

- The Local Newspaper: Even small communities typically have some form of a newspaper. It may only go into circulation once a week, but that will serve your purposes. If the publication is not available online then the local library likely has back issues of it available.

- Important Gathering Spots: Every small town typically has a location where the "old timers" hang out to drink coffee. If you can find that location (and the options are usually quite limited in a small town) they will often be more than happy to socialize with you. They are the ears of the community and often the voice too. If you use this route, be sure to leave a good impression. But what about in larger areas? The coffee shop route doesn't really work... You can hang out at Starbucks all day without accomplishing your goals. Still, there are locations where a great deal about the local schools and community can be learned such as City Council, Chamber Of Commerce, and Board Of Education meetings.

- Connections: You may not know anyone that lives in the town, but you likely know someone who knows someone. Put your contacts to work. Ask for a quick overview of what is going on in the community. Make sure that the contact is reliable. Misinformation is not going to be helpful. If you think this person will be doing any "campaigning" for you to obtain a job, they had better be a respected individual within their community. The town fool is not your best advocate.

Do your homework. The information you will gain and the background it will provide are vital. Knowledge is power and this power will enable you to stand out from the crowd.

"Spectacular achievement is always preceded by unspectacular preparation."
~ Robert H. Schuller

Answering interview questions is like a game of chess; you want to make each move count. Every statement should serve a purpose and it is not to simply get through the interview, but to outshine the competition. Every answer should build on the one before it, so you continue to mount a case for yourself as the best candidate for the job. Here are strategies to help you achieve that goal:

- **Strategy #1: Be Specific** - Generalized answers during an interview will get you nowhere. They are unmemorable and do nothing to further the possibility that you will obtain the job. A shining example? When the question is asked at an interview, "Why do you want to be a teacher?" and the applicant responds with, "Because I love kids." *Really? We thought you hated kids! Since you love them we'd better hire you on the spot.* All sarcasm aside, there are better ways to answer these types of questions. Some inquiries will provide a natural path to specific answers such as questions that start with: "Give me an example of...." Some will require a bit more creativity on your part.

- **Strategy #2: Be Memorable** – Many applicants who are interviewed blend in with the crowd. They do nothing to distinguish themselves and are forgotten the moment they walk out the door. Others, be it through their personality, the stories they tell, the attitude they bring or numerous other possibilities, make themselves memorable to their audience. They remain fresh in everyone's minds long after the last candidate has been interviewed. Will you be remembered?

- **Strategy #3: Show That You've Done Your Homework** - Work facts that you have learned about the district into your answers. It will demonstrate to employers that you are prepared and cared enough to research the situation prior to arriving.

- **Strategy #4: Be Professional** - Don't forget that you are interviewing for a serious position. Show everyone that you are capable of carrying yourself in a professional manner. It's fine if you are a funny person and want to use humor to your advantage during the interview, but don't cross the line. It is okay if you are a relaxed person, but don't seem so casual that you present an air of apathy. Gauge your audience to determine what is acceptable and what isn't.

- **Strategy #5: Present Well Thought Out Answers** - What happens if you get hit with a tough question that stumps you? There are one of three reactions that typically occur in this situation:

  - The candidate rushes through and gives a poor response.
  - The candidate does nothing and sits with a "deer in the headlights" expression.
  - The candidate pauses for a moment, thinks, and then gives a reasonable answer.

  The last option is the desirable choice. It's okay to take a moment to gather your thoughts. That is permissible within the unwritten interview rules. Also, if you need to buy some time, there is nothing wrong with repeating the question. Just don't do it every time or you will look foolish. Another solid tactic if you're befuddled on a question is to ask for further clarification. "Are you asking about conflict among students, teachers or both?" It shows you are listening and helps to get to the heart of the question as well. Once again, use it sparingly or it could backfire. What if you still need more time? Instead of spouting off something wild, we would recommend being honest. "I'd like to think about that question for a moment, would you mind if we come back to it?" While it may not be as impressive as responding with a solid answer, it will show the employer that you think before you act. Plus, you'll save yourself from saying something that you would later regret. Just make sure that when the question is asked for a second time you're ready for it.

- **Strategy #6: Monitor Your Pace** – This strategy is referring to the interview as a whole, not one specific question. Some candidates get in such a hurry that they will zip through the entire interview. Their nerves become frazzled the moment they walk in. Slow down and appear cool and collected (even if it's the farthest thing from the truth). Being nervous is perfectly natural.

- **Strategy #7: Give Short And Substantial Answers** - On the opposite end of the spectrum from "quick" answers, don't let your responses drone on indefinitely. Give an answer with some meat to it and then put the ball back in the interviewer's court. Watch closely for clues by "reading" your interviewers. If their body language indicates that you are speaking for too long, make an adjustment. You certainly don't want to give a ten-minute response to one question if the interview is only scheduled to last thirty minutes. If a candidate is boring during a short interview then no one wants to know how tiresome they could become during the course of an entire school year.

- **Strategy #8: Pay Attention** - Interviews are hard work. Depending on the format, you may have to be on top of your game from twenty minutes to half a day. If you want to give quality responses, you are going to need to be locked in to what the interviewer is saying. You can't text message an answer later, take a timeout to go ponder the situation or respond with an email tomorrow. You're going to have to focus and be ready to communicate quickly and concisely. The following techniques will help you to stay tuned in:

- *Specificity* - Repeat part of the question in your response to hone in on the content of the question. For instance, "What is your greatest strength?" could be answered with, *"My greatest strength is the ability to sit through an interview and pretend as if it is enjoyable."* Probably not the best example, but you get the idea.
- *Awareness* - What if you were the interviewer? What would you want to hear? Think questions through from the perspective of the employer. Why are they asking that question and what type of response is desired?
- *Focus* - This is not the time to show off your multitasking abilities. Focus only on the interview and lose the distractions. Your cell phone, shopping list, personal issues, and anything else not directly involved with the task at hand should be put on the back burner.

- **Strategy #9: Be Proactive** - Employers do not want people who wait for disaster to strike and then put a bandage on it. They want employees who fix problems before they occur. When issues arise (and they inevitably will) your boss will want you to get to the root of it and find out how to ensure that it will not happen again. Make it known that you are someone who takes the initiative to fix problems before they happen.

- **Strategy #10: Know Your Resume And Cover Letter** – Some people make claims they can't back up. Some even make statements in their resume and cover letter that are so far fetched that they don't even know the meaning. If you believe what is on your resume and cover letter this should not be a problem. It is a synopsis of your professional career and you should be knowledgeable and proud of your accomplishments. Remember what your true experiences are so you won't stumble through your interview.

By adhering to these ten simple strategies during your interview you can outperform a good percentage of the competition. In the next section we will show you how to take each of the strategies from theory to practice.

Sample Questions And Responses

"During a job interview, when they ask: 'What is your worst quality?', I always say: 'Flatulence.' That way I get my own office."
~ Dan Thompson

What follows are a number of sample interview questions and a breakdown of how to respond. Each will be broken into four sections:

- Question - An interview question will be stated.

- Quality Response - A quality response to the question will be shared.

- What To Watch For - Potential pitfalls will be explored.

- Something To Consider - One of the strategies from the previous section will be examined further.

In total there are ten questions. The questions and strategies are aligned with the strategies from the previous section (question number one utilizes strategy number one and so on). Many of you will want more guidance and examples than these questions can provide. There are extra questions in the appendix at the back of the book as well as an extensive collection of questions on our website at www.nelb.info.

Remember that the sample responses below are not to be used verbatim. We do not want your answers to sound scripted. With careful thought and consideration you can create quality responses that exemplify your style and personality.

Question #1: What is your biggest strength?

Quality Response: Just recently, my principal told me that she thought my people skills were phenomenal. She cited an example of how I handled an interesting situation during my first year of teaching. I was one of three second grade teachers and my two grade level colleagues couldn't stand each other; they didn't even like being in the same room! With time, patience, and the willingness to listen, I built a trusting relationship with both of these individuals. With me as the neutral third party, we managed to come together as a team. I won't try to convince you that they have the world's most harmonious relationship today, but they've gone from a toxic partnership to a productive one and I'm pleased to know that I played a part in that.

What To Watch For: There is no excuse to come unprepared for this common interview question. Don't stumble through a response. Your answer should be preloaded and ready to go, but not to the point it sounds rehearsed.

Something To Consider (Strategy #1: Be Specific): Too often people pick a generic response and leave it at that. "I'm a people person" is not an adequate answer to this question. What does that response tell the person conducting the interview? *That you don't hate people?* That's nice to know, but it doesn't add anything to the interview and does not increase your chances of being hired. Give them something to chew on! Why serve up an appetizer when you can place a delectable main course in front of them?

Question #2: How do you handle discipline?

Quality Response: I believe that the entire point of discipline is not to punish a child, but to help them learn from their mistakes. If a child is in violation of a minor rule then I will typically give them one opportunity to rectify the situation by saying, "I see that you are choosing to (whatever the behavior is). This is against our rules. You can choose to do it again if you want, but that will result in a consequence." If they choose to comply and abstain from the behavior in the future, then we move on. If they repeat the behavior immediately or choose to repeat it again after a short lapse, then I will assign a natural consequence to them. I will not get into conflicts with students over discipline. They can choose to follow the rules or they can choose a consequence, but the choice is theirs to make. I simply facilitate the outcome and help with the learning process.

What To Watch For: Stating that you frequently seek out help or send children to the principal's office demonstrates that you are incapable of handling discipline on your own. Show that you have a firm grasp over classroom management. If you cannot manage your students it will eliminate your chances of being hired; no one likes picking up the slack for an individual who has lost control of their class.

Something To Consider (Strategy #2: Be Memorable): How can you take this from generic to memorable? Tell about a personal experience that you've had with a student who is viewed as a discipline problem. Maybe it is a child that no one else was having success with, but you were able to reach. It could be a funny story, or a heartwarming "Ahhh...." moment that tugs on everyone's heartstrings. If you've got a story that stands out for this question, don't be afraid to use it.

Question #3: Can you please describe what your classroom will look like?

Quality Response: The desks would be arranged in groups of four so cooperative work would be easier to facilitate. However, with mobile furniture we could rearrange the desks into a circle or whatever format would best suit the needs of our current activity. Books and resources that meet the needs of all students would be plentiful. Student work would be visible throughout the room to instill pride and develop a sense of belonging. The lesson objective would be clearly posted so the main concept was clear. Students in my room would be highly engaged and excited about learning.

What To Watch For: There are many different areas that could be discussed within this one question, but you don't want to speak indefinitely. Give the interviewer enough examples to show that you're knowledgable and then determine if they still want more information. "I could discuss my room all day, but I don't want to bore you. Would you like for me to talk about any more specifics in my classroom: technology, arrangement of books, posters, centers, etc?"

Something To Consider (Strategy #3: Show That You've Done Your Homework): This could be a wonderful place to demonstrate that you've studied the school/district. "From what I've read online, your district seems to have a vested interest in cooperative learning. I think that by arranging my desks in groups of four I will easily be able to incorporate a number of cooperative learning strategies into my instruction." Show them that you care about this position and went the extra mile to be prepared.

Question #4: Are you comfortable working with people from diverse backgrounds?

Quality Response: Absolutely. I love what different cultures can bring to a working environment and have found that there are tremendous learning experiences to be gained when numerous backgrounds are represented. I taught at a school that had a high percentage of students whose primary language was not English. It was a fascinating experience to see people from different languages and cultures learn so much from one another.

What To Watch For: If you are asked this question in an interview, it is likely because the school is highly diverse. You will only know what types of diversity the school is working with if you have done your research. Is there a challenging special education population? Or a high percentage of students who speak a second language? Maybe there is a wide range of socioeconomic statuses or possibly the majority of the school is composed of one (or multiple) minority groups? If you've studied the school you will already know the answer and can respond to the question appropriately.

Something To Consider (Strategy #4: Be Professional): Candidates can be unprofessional when responding to any question, but inquiries about diversity have a strong tendency to create issues for those that are unprepared. Generalizations, stereotypes, and even flat out racism are just some of the faux pas that we've seen committed. These are all surefire ways to end your chances of obtaining a job.

Question #5: Can you share an example of when you've worked through a conflict with a coworker?

Quality Response: Two years ago I had a disagreement with a teacher on my grade level team. I felt that we were losing instructional time during our hallway transitions. I wanted to implement some activities that we could incorporate while we waited. The other teacher had the valid concern that this may create too much noise in the hallway. We worked through this dilemma and found a way to incorporate learning activities in the hallway that had no potential for disturbing other classes. It was a mild disagreement, but it caused us both to think about the situation and see the validity in each other's argument. More importantly, it helped to benefit the students. We still utilize the hallway lessons to this day.

What To Watch For: Facts can be quickly separated from fiction by an experienced employer. If you were to respond with, "I've never had a problem with a coworker," the employer's likely line of thought will be, *"Really? Is that right? Well, we've got a historical first here, ladies and gentlemen. The first employee who has never had a problem with any coworkers!"* Be believable and find a happy medium. You've had small problems that were resolved and you learned from them.

Something To Consider (Strategy #5: Present Well Thought Out Answers): Questions like this have numerous factors and can often create issues. You don't want to rush into your response and give an answer you regret. *"Well there was this teacher Bill....we hated each other with a passion! Our conflict was resolved on the day I finally got him fired."* At the same time, you don't want to sit there and say nothing. Take your time, weigh the outcomes and go with your gut.

Question #6: How do you handle change?

Quality Response: I can readily adapt, especially when it is best for kids. A principal once asked me to switch grade levels because my talents were needed with another group. While it certainly wasn't my preference, I approached the challenge with a positive attitude and made it work. Within a short time I was not only enjoying the experience immensely, but growing rapidly as I learned a new curriculum and effective strategies for working with a different age group.

What To Watch For: Change is often feared. Many people also handle it poorly. Regardless of how those in our field choose to cope, education and change go hand in hand. If you are someone who spends your energy fighting what's new it will be a full time battle. Do not reveal to your prospective employer that you are someone who will fight change. Creating a better learning experience for students is difficult enough without having to drag the naysayers along every step of they way. Be someone who is willing to take a chance if it means a potential benefit for those around you.

Something To Consider (Strategy #6: Monitor Your Pace): For whatever reason, be it pressure, nerves, or simply not understanding what is at stake, many candidates feel that a brief, uninformative answer will be sufficient. It isn't. The answer to this question is not, "I'm good at change." This response adds nothing to the conversation and does not further your chances of being hired. When candidates repeatedly answer in this fashion, an interview can be over in a matter of minutes. This makes for an awkward situation, but it is a relief for the interviewer because they can get on to the next candidate (who hopefully has something substantial to say).

Question #7: Why would you be a good candidate for this position?

Quality Response: I feel that my skill set is perfectly aligned with the needs of the building. There are a high number of Spanish speaking students here and I'm currently learning to speak Spanish. The school did not make AYP in mathematics last year and my concentration in college was math. There are a substantial number of students receiving free and reduced lunches and I have had extensive training in working with students from poverty. My training and experience have prepared me for the challenges of this position.

What To Watch For: Once again, if you have done your homework you are going to ace this question. It's difficult to know what would make you a good candidate for the position unless you know the specific needs of the building. Maybe you have desirable certifications, knowledge of a language common among the students, or experience dealing with a weakness implied by the data. If you don't know the specific details, you will only be able to answer with generalities.

Something To Consider (Strategy #7: Give Short And Substantial Answers): When answering this question (or many others) the candidate has the potential to ramble on and on for a lengthy amount of time. Do you think that is what the interviewer is looking for? Obviously not. They have other questions to ask and other candidates to interview. You don't want an answer that is too brief, such as, "I'd be a good candidate because I'm a hard worker." At the same time, you don't want to talk for so long that the interviewer begins to view you as a liability.

Question #8: Can you give an example of a time when you tried a classroom management technique that did not work?

Quality Response: While student teaching I made the mistake of reprimanding a fifth grade student in front of his peers. He, of course, felt the need to defend himself, so he lashed back at me with a verbal assault. I calmed the situation down and quietly asked him to join me in the hall so we could continue the discussion in private. When it was just the two of us things went a lot smoother. I learned a valuable lesson about discipline with dignity that day.

What To Watch For: You need to share a mistake at this point, but it is okay to select a minor one. Don't pick the biggest gaffe that you've ever committed. This isn't the best time for the story about how you burnt the school to the ground trying to prove a point to your students. Find a story that demonstrates a minor flaw and roll with it.

Something To Consider (Strategy #8: Pay Attention): What do you think is going through the interviewer's head when this question is asked? What kind of response is desired? It's doubtful that they're looking for you to respond with some form of denial such as, "I've never had a technique not work. My classroom management is flawless." They'll know that's a lie before you're done spinning it. They likely want to know that you are someone who can recognize shortcomings and has the ability to grow from them.

Question #9: What would you do if a student constantly blurted out during class?

Quality Response: I'd start by talking to the student and modeling the correct way to gain attention in class. I'd make sure to show specific praise when the correct techniques were utilized by saying something like, "I like the way you raised your hand to get my attention. What would you like to share with the class?" If that did not work then we could try more intense interventions.

What To Watch For: Start with the simplest solutions first. In this case you wouldn't want to jump to immediately putting the student on a behavior plan or pondering if he/she is hyperactive. It's just blurting. It's a common problem, so handle it as such.

Something To Consider (Strategy #9: Be Proactive): The real question here is *why* is the student blurting? Are they seeking attention? Or possibly extra recognition? Maybe they're restless and need an outlet for their energy. If the cause can be determined, then it can also be resolved. Meet the child's needs and the blurting will become a non-issue.

Question #10: What are your feelings on state assessments and AYP?

Quality Response: From the looks of things I should probably be asking you that question. You've seen your test scores. They're amazing. You made huge leaps in math and reading last year and met AYP once again. From what I can see, you've never failed to make AYP. Given the extremely diverse demographics of this building, including 60% of students whom are ELL and over 90% are below the poverty line, that is absolutely amazing to me. Now, as for my personal thoughts on state assessments and AYP, I believe that it has had both positive and negative effects. It has helped to close achievement gaps, but at the same time it has left numerous educators teaching to the test. Like it or not, the age of accountability is here to stay.

What To Watch For: Even if you are a staunch opponent of No Child Left Behind, state assessments, and Adequate Yearly Progress, this is not the time to try to advocate for the elimination of high stakes testing. There are strong supporters for these concepts and your interviewers may be among them. Show that you are knowledgeable of heated subjects such as this one, but stay neutral at the same time.

Something To Consider (Strategy #10: Know Your Resume And Cover Letter): Reference your experience when it is beneficial. It should be stated on your resume already so they can review it if desired. On this question you may have some specific item from your career that you can share. *"As I've noted on my resume, my students have received the standard of excellence on their state assessments at two different schools. That is the same expectation I will have for my future students as well."*

Chapter Seven: Interview Preparation

What To Wear

*"Never wear a backwards baseball cap to an interview
unless applying for the job of umpire."*
~ Dan Zevin

First impressions are extremely important. Before the first word comes out of your mouth, employers will already be sizing you up. One of the factors they will use to do that is your appearance.

When giving you dress tips for an interview, we're going to assume that you know the obvious. If you need to be told that nose rings and tattoos are a bad idea, or that flip-flops are not ideal footwear, then you probably need more help than we can provide.

Wear an outfit that will present you as a professional. If you're wondering if something is appropriate, then don't wear it. Rules and opinions will vary depending on who you ask, but overdressing for the part is better than under dressing. Recently a young man in a suit interviewed for one of our paraprofessional openings. Did he need to wear a suit? Not necessarily for a job of that caliber. Was he docked any points for it? Absolutely not. It was an impressive and well noted effort.

What if you don't own any professional clothes? What if you don't know how to tie a tie? What if your nicest pair of shoes has a swoosh on the side? All of these situations are easily fixable. Buy some professional clothes! Even if you're broke, you can find a sale or even purchase something second hand that is still current and practically new. If you don't know what looks professional or how to construct an appropriate outfit, there are plenty of people who are willing to help you. Be careful who you pick; you don't want help from someone who is just as clueless as you but fails to realize it. If your mom routinely wears ugly holiday themed sweaters, she is probably not your ideal person for assistance. Still can't find anyone? Not an issue. Walk into a store, find the sharpest dressed salesperson and be honest with him or her. You need a professional outfit for an interview, you have no clue what to buy, and you want to spend "x" amount of dollars.

Your other consideration besides professionalism is comfort. Don't pick something that makes you miserable and thus jeopardizes your ability to shine at the interview. You want to look good and feel good at the same time. Think about the last time that you wore something truly uncomfortable. How did it make you feel? It's likely that whatever negative emotions it produced were also apparent in your attitude. Feeling good and looking good go hand in hand. Take the time to pick out the right outfit and you'll have one less thing to worry about.

While not a clothing item, poor hygiene or cleanliness can wreck even the perfect outfit (and the entire interview for that matter).

Some specific tips to consider:

Men

- Suit (not mandatory for all jobs, but preferred; choose navy or dark gray)
- Slacks (if a suit is not selected)
- Long sleeved shirt
- Tie (conservative pattern)
- Belt
- Dark socks
- Dress shoes (leather, matched to belt, polished)
- Freshly cut hair
- Well shaven or groomed facial hair (limited or no aftershave)
- Trimmed and cleaned nails
- Limited jewelry (no more than a watch and ring)

Women

- Suit (solid color)
- Skirt/pants and blouse (appropriate length and comfort while sitting)
- Clean, polished, conservative shoes
- Freshly cut hair
- Light (or no) perfume and makeup
- Manicured nails
- Limited jewlery

Clothes for both men and women should fit well and should be clean and pressed. Leave all the accessories at home or in your car. There is no need for your phone or drink. If you choose to use a portfolio, bring it along. Everything else can be left behind.

Ask someone for an honest opinion once everything is selected. If your husband is simply trying to avoid an argument or if your wife is hesitant of offending you, then they are not your best bets.

When it comes to interviews, you are what you wear. You have to make sure to dress for the part. Take this opportunity to shine from the inside out. When you look good, you feel good, and when you feel good, you will have more confidence.

Chapter Seven: Interview Preparation

Practice, Practice, Practice

"An ounce of practice is worth more than tons of preaching."
~ Mahatma Ghandi

You will only improve your interview skills through practice. Over-preparation is key; to earn a job you are going to have to outwork the competition. One simple way to accomplish this is by keeping a list of interview questions in your possession (there is an ample supply available at www.nelb.info) and quizzing yourself whenever you have a free moment. Another excellent idea is to make sure that you are current on hot topics and trends in education. Not only can you work these concepts into your answers, but if a question is specifically about one of these topics, you'll be prepared. There are numerous educational magazines and websites that you can read to stay up to date. For an overview of some items that are worth knowing, look at the list in our appendix called "Trending Topics In Education." You can skim it and do a search online for any items with which you are unfamiliar. While beefing up your knowledge base and practicing questions by yourself will be an immense help, the most efficient practice technique is a mock interview.

Mock interviews are essential to your preparation. Through someone else's eyes you can discover a lot about what you are doing well and what needs work. The most important part of this process is finding the appropriate person to help you. There are two criteria that stand above the rest when making this selection; experience and honesty.

The experience piece is obvious. Those with experience in education (particularly those responsible for hiring) will be able to give a more realistic interview and better feedback than someone who has no real life experience in the field. That's not to say that there is nothing to be gained if the best help you can find has less than ideal experience. If the person has sound judgment (and they are not competing for the same job you are) they should still be able to provide constructive feedback.

The individual conducting the mock interview must also be willing to honestly inform you of your flaws. Selecting someone who will sugar coat your weaknesses will do nothing to improve your performance. It may make you feel better momentarily, but it won't improve your probability of landing a job.

With the appropriate person selected, you will be ready to conduct your mock interview. An extremely powerful tip of which most job seekers fail to take advantage is to record the session. When using this technique, it makes sense to record the audio and video. Much of the interviewer's perception will be based on visuals as well, so use your camcorder or laptop to get the full picture. Analyze the interview when you are done. Look at all aspects, not just the quality of your answers. Examine the rate of speech, clarity, body language, posture and expressions. Determine what you need to work on and get it fixed.

Something else that can be done for a more effective practice session is to simulate the format of an upcoming interview as closely as possible. How can you truly know what to expect so you are preparing correctly? As we've stated before, education is a small world. You'll need to utilize your network to see what information can be obtained. Find a way to make casual inquiries about the interview. What is the typical format used by the district? Who usually conducts interviews? What kind of questions are normally asked? If you have some background knowledge in advance, you can make your mock interviews more realistic. Practice doesn't make perfect. *Perfect* practice makes perfect.

Chapter Seven: Interview Preparation

Activities and Discussion

Welcome to the activities and discussion section for chapter seven. Everything you need to participate is located on the website that accompanies this book:

www.nelb.info

- In the Chapter Seven Forum you will find our "Interview Simulator". Pretend that you are in a real interview and see how you do. Share your thoughts afterwards.

- There is a great deal that can be learned from being the interviewer instead of the interviewee. It is a perspective switch that can be very enlightening. Find someone with whom to conduct a mock interview and put yourself in the role of interviewer. Contribute any insight gained to the Chapter Seven Forum thread called "Perspective Switch".

- The opening story in this chapter shared an experience that a principal uses in all of his interviews. Do you have any stories that tell about you as an educator? What are they? Share one in the Chapter Seven Forum in the thread "Interview Stories".

- Have you found an interview question that is giving you trouble? Sometimes it is difficult to find the right answer. Post a challenging interview question in the Chapter Seven Forum under "Challenging Questions" and answer a question from another user.

* In addition to your own thoughts, you are welcome to respond to the posts of other users. Please make sure to protect the private information of others at all times on our website. Use pseudonyms and eliminate any contact information for individuals referenced. Thank you for your cooperation.

Chapter Eight

The Interview

Great Blunders In Job Search History

Honest Abe goes a step too far.

Three of the most interesting interviews I have ever conducted all happened on the same day. Our district was in need of a new industrial arts teacher so three candidates who had recently applied were selected to interview.

The first interview was going well and I decided to take the gentleman out for a tour of the town. This was standard procedure since it is a small community and as superintendent I wanted all potential hires to get a feel for the surroundings. As we were driving around pursuing homes that were available for rent, the man kept inquiring, "How many bedrooms does that house have?" After the question had been repeated several times I finally asked, "Why so much curiosity about the number of bedrooms?" My hope was that he would be bringing a family full of children with him and planned on enrolling them at our schools. Instead I was shocked when he responded with, "My wife and I just got a divorce and I don't want her thinking that my daughter is sleeping in the same room as me." That comment was disturbing enough that I knew the interview was over. I also knew a drink was going to be in order when I arrived at home.

The second interview was with a gentleman who had worked in a neighboring district for several years. After the customary greetings, I began to ask him my first question when he interrupted with, "Let me stop you right there." At that point he threw his portfolio on my desk and said, "I think my work speaks for itself." He then tipped his chair back and slid his hand down his pants (a la Al Bundy). Needless to say there was no need for a tour of the community.

After abruptly dismissing the second candidate I moved on to the third interview. One look and I began to wonder what sins I had committed against the interview gods to be punished in this manner. The man had severely disheveled hair, torn blue jeans, a wildly unkempt mustache and smelled strongly of cologne with a hint of cigarette smoke. He then sat down and we had an amazing conversation that centered entirely on students for the next two hours. Guess it's true; you can't always judge a book by its cover. I hired him on the spot!

~ Terry, Superintendent

Types Of Interviews

"In most cases, the best strategy for a job interview is to be fairly honest, because the worst thing that can happen is that you won't get the job and will spend the rest of your life foraging for food in the wilderness and seeking shelter underneath a tree or the awning of a bowling alley that has gone out of business."
~ Lemony Snicket

There are several different interview formats that you may encounter during your job search. A basic list would include small group, one on one, rotating, phone, and screening interviews. To briefly expand on each of these:

- Small Group - This is typically the most common interview format. The group will likely be composed of people who will work closely with the selected candidate, but there are numerous individuals who could be involved (academic coaches, vertical teams, support staff, or even teams consisting entirely of administrators).

- One On One - This is usually the supervisor (interviewer) and the candidate (interviewee). It has become less and less common as an emphasis on collaboration has emerged. Administrators also feel that their staff will be more supportive of a new hire if they are involved in the process.

- Rotating - In this format the candidate is interviewed by multiple groups. This is more common when hiring an administrator, but it can be utilized at all levels. It involves interviewing with two or more groups, one after the other. Some common groups are administrators, teachers, and parents.

- Screening - These types of interviews are common at job fairs. They are quick, informal and are used so that both parties can learn about one another. Two important things to remember when visiting a job fair or other gathering with short screening interviews are:
  - come prepared with resumes to share
  - be ready to impress; with an extremely short time frame to grasp an interviewer's attention, how will you leave an impression?

- Phone - When looking at the possibility of hiring a candidate from out of state or a similarly distant location, phone interviews are sometimes utilized. They could be in any of the formats listed above (speaker phones would be used for a group). Before you interview by phone:
  - locate a quiet spot to interview
  - have all of your information easily accessible (spreading it out at eye level is a great tactic; it keeps you from shuffling papers and having to

constantly look down; you can use a bulletin board or tape your documents to the wall in front of you)
  ○ interview from a location where reception will not be an issue (landlines without call waiting are ideal)
  ○ determine whether you will perform better while sitting or standing
  ○ let those conducting the interview "hear" you smile; a positive attitude can be conveyed through tone

- Lesson Demonstration - As one component of the interview, some districts may want to see you in action. Although uncommon, this is not unheard of. They may request a live lesson or a recorded one submitted by DVD or email. If you are asked to do a model lesson make sure it is one you have done before. It should be one of your best lessons; this is not the time for average. Leave your audience clamoring for more.

Whichever type of format is selected, those conducting the interview will either use formal questioning, informal questioning or a combination of both. Formal questioning is simply when the employer has a set list of questions to ask and sticks to them. During group interviews, those asking the questions will often take turns. Informal questioning is when the employer asks whatever questions come to mind. A combination of both methods can be used. This involves a set list of questions, but the applicant's responses determine the follow up questions and what path the interview will take.

Regardless of the format, you will be fine if you stick to the techniques we have discussed throughout this book. It doesn't matter if you are interviewing with one person or a whole room full of them. If you have an interview, then the group was already impressed enough by your resume that they wanted to hear more from you. Your goal during the interview is to do a good enough job selling yourself that they are further enticed and want to seal the deal. Remember that you aren't just selling yourself from the moment you shake hands with the person leading the interview; you are making your pitch from the moment you walk in the door. Treat everyone with the utmost respect and courtesy from step one. If the secretary and other people you encounter aren't impressed with you, they'll make sure that those on the interview committee know about it. Leave no one in doubt. *You* are the best candidate for the job.

Chapter Eight: The Interview

Questions And Answers

"I had a job interview at an insurance company once and the lady said 'Where do you see yourself in five years?' and I said 'Celebrating the fifth year anniversary of you asking me this question.'"
~ *Mitch Hedberg*

When it comes to interview questions, some people are naturals, some people need more preparation and some people simply *think* they are naturals.

Regardless of which category you fall into, preparation will be helpful. This isn't a scripted play and there is no way to know exactly what will be asked. If you try to memorize lines in advance, it will likely sound rehearsed. Although memorization isn't the goal, preparation is. Know what you want to speak about and who you want to focus on (hopefully students).

To briefly review what was stated in chapter seven, your answers should be:

- specific
- memorable
- researched
- professional
- well thought out
- paced appropriately
- substantial, not sustained
- focused
- proactive
- supported by your resume

Lists of specific interview questions and how to handle each of them can be found in both chapter seven and in the appendix. There is also an extensive collection of questions available online at www.nelb.info under "Resources." With dedicated practice you can work to prepare yourself for nearly any inquiry a potential employer may have.

The first question is of the utmost importance, so be prepared. Walk in with shoulders squared and give a firm handshake with plenty of eye contact. The employer will open up with a remark to get the conversation started. More often than not it will be, "Can you tell us a little about yourself?"

Rest assured that the appropriate answer is not, *"It was a dark and windy day on the morn of August 28, 1983. My mother was anxious, but eerily calm. It was to her great relief when I, a large baby at nine and a half pounds, 21 inches in length, was finally welcomed into the world...*

Give the condensed version. There's no guarantee that you'll be asked this question, but it is likely, so be prepared. What are the key points that you would like to discuss? Is it a unique story about how you arrived in education? Do you have an interesting background that would intrigue those conducting the interview? Can you work tactful humor into your response, thus easing your nerves and the overall mood of the interview? Think it through and you'll find what is right for you.

What are other commonly used ice breakers? There are no guarantees, but some typical ones are:

- Some weather we're having out there, huh?
    - Generic weather comments are great filler in interviews and all walks of life.

- Did you find the building okay?
    - Answer in the affirmative even if it is a blatant lie. You want to display competence from the get go.

- How are you?
    - There are two approaches here. You can take the extremely positive road, "I'm great, how are you?" or, depending on your current state, you can also say, "To be honest, I'm a little nervous." There is nothing wrong with enthusiasm or honesty. The former shows that you are a positive person, while the latter says that you may not be at 100% right now because of your level of excitement. Don't give the unenthusiastic response of "I'm okay" or "so-so" and definitely don't stoop to a negative response. We want people working for us that are "Wonderful" or "Outstanding", not people who respond to this question with, "It's almost Friday." Set the tone for the interview from the beginning and reap the rewards later.

There are also some sure-fire things to avoid when answering questions. Whatever you do, avoid these obvious pitfalls:

- Family Plans: Do not discuss your desire to have a baby in the near future. If you just became pregnant or want to be pregnant soon, save that information for later. Working around maternity leave and the needs of new parents is an inconvenience for employers and while most will never admit it to you, it is easier to not have to deal with it at all.

- Religion: You are entitled to your personal beliefs. If you are a devoutly religious individual, then more power to you. However, your interview is not the time for a sermon. Leave your religious beliefs off of school grounds (unless of course you are applying at a private school with ideas that mirror your own). With society's large variety of faiths (and people who claim no religion at all) you stand a good chance of offending someone with a discussion about religion during an interview.

- Politics: Decisions made by politicians can have drastic effects on our educational landscape. Many people have very strong feelings about certain parties and passionate dedications to one side or another. Interviews are not the time to voice these opinions. The odds of you having the same political mindset as an entire interview committee are slim to none.

- Casualness: Being relaxed is one thing, being overly casual is another altogether. Use correct titles such as Mr., Miss, Ms., Mrs., and Dr. as well as sir and ma'am. These are not your buddies, they are your potential bosses and coworkers. Treat them as such.

- Sharing That You Relocate Frequently: Many people move frequently for a variety of reasons (a spouse's line of work being one of the most common). This is often outside of an individual's control, however, please note that it takes an enormous amount of effort to train a teacher and prepare them for all the nuances of a specific school. Employers don't want to hire someone that they believe will relocate in short order. If you move frequently it will be demonstrated by your resume, there is no need to remind anyone of this fact during an interview.

- Employment Difficulties: If you tell everyone that this is your ninth interview and you still aren't having any luck, they're immediately going to begin wondering why the other eight districts didn't want you.

- Excuses: Save them. Employers want people who can take responsibility for their own actions.

- Negativity: Leave it in your car before entering the building. Negativity breeds more negativity. Complain to yourself on the way home from the interview if needed; no one else wants to hear it.

Avoiding these items should be easy. Be well aware of your surroundings and use common sense. You've worked too hard for silly mistakes to blow this opportunity.

Positive Posture

"The language of the body is the key that can unlock the soul."
~ Konstantin Stanislavsky

Get up and find a mirror right now; bring the book with you. Go on, *now!* We know that you're still sitting there reading this. We'll wait....

There? Good. Slump down into your droopiest posture, think about something negative or frustrating and take a look at yourself. What do you see? Now, think those positive thoughts, square your shoulders and lift up nice and tall. Notice a difference? Of course you do. Whoever is conducting your interview will too. You're going to have a million other things on your mind when you enter the interview, but don't forget about your body language.

Sit up straight and proud. Don't lean all over the table as if it is Saturday morning and you're about to fall into your breakfast. Have some poise. Make eye contact and if you can remember nothing else, *smile!* If you're unsure of what to do, mirror the interviewer's style. If you follow their lead it will put you both at ease. Listen with your whole body. What does your posture say? Is it, "I am interested in what you are saying," or "I would rather be anywhere but here"?

Avoid the obvious pitfalls. You know that you shouldn't lean back, unfasten your belt or begin digging around inside your ear to satisfy an itch. You're certainly not so clueless that you are going to smack some gum, light up a smoke or start playing with your cell phone. But also stay away from other nervous tendencies like hair twirling, foot tapping, finger drumming, nail biting, repeatedly crossing/uncrossing arms/legs and especially yawning. If you're bored to the point that you need a good yawn, it might be a good idea to call things off and save everyone some time.

Look confident (even if you're not) and capture your audience with your aura. Sit up straight, make eye contact and focus. Lean in to give them the signal that you're intrigued (even if it's a fib). If you make the interviewers believe that's how you feel, it will be good enough. Perception is reality!

Chapter Eight: The Interview

Be Willing To Laugh At Yourself

"Laugh at yourself first, before anyone else can."
~ Elsa Maxwell

"Kids don't know how much you care until they care how much you know." Read that again if you didn't catch it. Doesn't make any sense, huh? That's because it's supposed to be, "Kids don't care how much you know until they know how much you care." The first version is the gem that one of us decided to unload during an interview and it sounded *really* awkward.

So what were the options at that point? Cruise on and pretend like it didn't happen? Ask for a mulligan? Give up and walk out? Possible, but a different course of action was chosen. There was a pause, laugh, smile and a revised version before moving on with the interview. The next day the administrator who had been doing the interview called with a job offer.

Don't give up just because a mistake is made; they happen, get over it! What's the worst that could happen? You don't get the job? You already don't have the job, so you're no worse off! If nothing else, learn from the experience and move on. That's the value of making mistakes in the first place; you get the opportunity to learn from them! If you take yourself too seriously, no one will take you seriously at all.

"If you think hiring professionals is expensive, try hiring amateurs."
~ Red Adair

What is the interviewer up to during an interview? What are some of the tricks that are used? Common practices are:

- Pondering the Dynamics: Employers spend the majority of their time on one key question: How will you fit with the rest of the staff? Your answers to questions will help them to determine if there is chemistry. If you seem like someone who will be a good fit and solid contributor, you may have a shot. If you aren't the right fit, then your job search will likely continue.

- Looking for Information: There are certain questions that interviewers are not permitted to ask due to legal restrictions. That's why the question, "Tell me a little bit about yourself" is so common. Employers aren't going to ask you about the personal details of your life, but they are hopeful that you will share voluntarily. Connecting on a personal level is an important factor. No connection may mean no job. Find one and establish it.

- Silently Biding Our Time: As interviewers we're often content to ride out your answers in silence during an interview. If you're going to hang yourself with a long response that goes further and further down a road that should not have been traveled, don't expect us to give you directions back to the main path. We're going to sit back and see where the journey takes us. So what's the solution if you find yourself on this wayward route? Be quiet, stop rambling and get back on track.

- Finding Out Who You Really Are: We're looking for all the clues and signs to see if you are competent, current on what is going on in education, positive, hard working and honest. We're also determining if you have the tools to do the job at hand right now or if you will need additional training.

- Making Our Decision: Not to scare you, but we typically know if we want to hire you within the first five minutes of the interview (and that's a conservative estimate). Come prepared to make a solid first impression, because we're sizing you up from the moment you walk in.

That's how we spend the majority of our time during the interview. Give us what we're looking for and the last item, "Making Our Decision" will become just that much easier.

What Questions Do You Have

"When you go in for a job interview, I think a good thing to ask is if they ever press charges."

~ Jack Handy

There are no guarantees on what will be asked at an interview. However, "What questions do you have?" will be the likely conclusion. We ask it every time, unless we are sure that the candidate is not a good fit for the job and are attempting to end the interview as soon as possible.

People regularly wonder what is appropriate to ask during this time. In our minds there is one response that stands out above all others as unacceptable:

"No. I don't have any questions."

This is absolutely, positively, a waste of a golden opportunity. You have the ability to take the interview in any direction you would like at this point. You can ask anything and set the tone for how the interview will close. So what should you say?

There are some topics to avoid. You don't want to ask about contract hours. What would you think if you were conducting an interview and a candidate asked about report and dismissal times for staff members? Even if unintended, it appears as if they are trying to determine the fewest amount of hours they can work within the limitations of a contract. Inquiries about sick and personal days are an equally poor choice. You might as well begin faking a cough if you are going to ask about days off during an interview. You won't need to call in sick though, because you won't be hired.

Some people wonder if asking how much the job pays is an appropriate question. We wouldn't recommend it. Think about it; is that really how you want to end the interview? What kind of message does it send if you leave with your focus on money instead of students? If they offer you the job they're going to tell you how much it would pay prior to you accepting anyway. Plus, if you did your homework, there was probably a salary schedule available online.

How can you take better advantage of your opportunity? With a question that displays your level of preparation:

- What would you say is your biggest accomplishment as a school?

- I've heard that you started a new reading series last year. What are your thoughts on it so far?

- I was examining your significant gains on the math portion of the state assessments last year. How was this accomplished?"

Specificity is the key. It shows that you are interested in this school. Do your homework and come prepared to finish strong. Ignorance is not an option.

This is a position where you may be working for a very long time. Is there other information that you need to know? During most of the interview the focus is on you, but now it is time to turn the tables. Remember, when you go to an interview, they aren't just interviewing you; you're interviewing them as well. However, don't ask so many questions that the employers become annoyed with you. Ask the few questions that are most interesting to you and let the interviewers wrap things up.

When you have asked your final question, the interview will draw to a close. Thank everyone for their time, shake hands once again and leave as gracefully as you entered. Remember, the interview is not officially over until you are back in the privacy of your own vehicle and heading home. Carry yourself appropriately.

Chapter Eight: The Interview

Activities and Discussion

Welcome to the activities and discussion section for chapter eight. Everything you need to participate is located on the website that accompanies this book:

www.nelb.info

- In the Chapter Eight Forum watch the videos in the "Mock Interview" thread and contribute your thoughts.

- There are a wide variety of bizarre interview questions out there. A couple of our favorites are, "If you could be any type of tree, what would you be?" and "How many educational acronyms can you name in thirty seconds? Go!" Share the craziest one you've come across in the Chapter Eight Forum under "Quirky Questions."

- Have you ever had an interview completely blow up in your face? Horror stories and interviews tend to go hand in hand. If you've had the misfortune to experience one of these moments (or know someone who has) please share the story in the Chapter Eight Forum under "Interview Insanity." Don't forget the aftermath; we want to know if there was a recovery or if it was a lost cause.

* In addition to your own thoughts, you are welcome to respond to the posts of other users. Please make sure to protect the private information of others at all times on our website. Use pseudonyms and eliminate any contact information for individuals referenced. Thank you for your cooperation.

Chapter Nine

Post Interview

Great Blunders In Job Search History

Casanova's thank you letter following his interview
crosses some professional boundaries.

Several years ago I saw a posting for an administrative opening that was very appealing to me. It was in a location that was desirable, the pay was good and the district had a solid reputation. I applied and was thrilled when I was contacted about visiting for an interview.

I arrived full of energy and excitement about the possibilities that lay before me. The interview was set up so I would meet with a group of the building's teachers, followed by a second session with several administrators. I walked in and the teachers were not all ready to begin. This was fine with me as it gave me a chance to mingle with those who were prepared. We had an informal conversation prior to any of their set interview questions. I was taken aback when the teachers began a verbal assault against the current administration.

By the time the question portion of the interview began, the whole process may as well have been over. The group's negative attitude had soured my feelings about the opportunity and it was apparent in my responses.

I finished with the teachers and had a poor experience with the administrators as well. Negativity seemed to permeate from the entire faculty. It was a disheartening experience to say the least.

I drove away rapidly, attempting to distance myself from the entire situation. I was glad the experience was over and I could put it behind me. Imagine my surprise when I was offered the job the next day.

So what did I do? Good location. Great money. Poor job. The decision was easy. I turned them down on the spot and haven't regretted it since. Life is too short to work in that type of environment. I want to surround myself with other people who love coming to work each day.

~ David, Principal

Thanking Your Prospective Employer

"Silent gratitude isn't much use to anyone."
~ *G. B. Stern*

What is the next step after completing an interview? Someone has just given you the opportunity to become gainfully employed. They have also taken time out of their busy day to meet with you. As a matter of common courtesy, you need to thank them. It shows good manners. Your mother would approve.

So what is the best way to go about this? People use phone calls and emails, but a handwritten note is the best approach. It won't be an inconvenience to the recipient like a phone call (since they can read it on their own time) and it is more personal and meaningful than an email could ever be. Keep it short, sweet, and grateful. An example would be:

Dear Mrs. Interviewer,

Thank you so much for taking the time out of your busy day to meet with me. I truly enjoyed getting to see the school and visit with your staff. It is apparent that you are all doing wonderful things for students. Thanks again for this opportunity.

Sincerely,

John Q. Applicant

"All great truths are simple in final analysis, and easily understood;
if they are not, they are not great truths."
~ Napoleon Hill

Every interview, regardless if you are offered the position or not, is a unique learning experience. After you've given your final handshakes and have a moment to reflect, consider:

- What went right?

- What went wrong?

- How will you do better next time?

Was there a question that stumped you? Analyze it and consider what you should have said. Were there awkward moments in the interview? What created them and how can they be avoided in the future? Was there something you could have done to be better prepared? Make a note of it and never let it create a stumbling block again.

Mistakes happen. That is life. It is how individuals choose to handle mistakes that separates successful people from the rest of the pack. Will you learn from failures or repeat them continually? The choice is yours.

Ultimately your analysis needs to end with one final question: Do you still want the job? Our current economy doesn't allow one to be as picky or selective as in the past. However, sometimes you can tell that a job simply isn't going to be a good fit. In those situations you have to ask yourself if it would be a good idea to accept the position if it is offered. Money is most certainly not everything. You have to factor happiness and satisfaction into the equation as well. Love for your job trumps a paycheck any day.

We have called each other after interviews and said, "There is no way that I would ever work there." Be it a difference in philosophy, a poor perception of the district's direction or simply a gut feeling that it wasn't a good match, there are times when you have to use a line from an old anti-drug slogan and "Just Say No."

This isn't to say that you shouldn't approach things with an open mind. We've both accepted positions that we viewed as less than ideal. Upon working at those jobs and getting to know the students and staff, we ended up not only enjoying them, but learning a great deal as well. Don't lock yourself out of opportunities because of a narrow vision. An open mind will open doors.

When The Job Is Offered/Denied

"The only place where success comes before work is in the dictionary."
~ Donald Kendall

If the administrator that interviewed you has any class at all (and some of them don't), you will be notified when they have selected a candidate. This notification will come via letter, email or (most commonly) a phone call. The message will share one of three things: they have chosen you, they have chosen someone else or they would like for you to come back for an additional interview.

If the employer tells you that you are their chosen candidate, congratulations! If you desire the job then you should graciously accept and inquire about what steps are next. On top of being thankful, please show a little enthusiasm. When offering a job to someone we expect to hear some excitement in their voice. When a selected candidate responds as if they have been contacted by a telemarketer about saving money on their insurance, it makes us wonder if we've made a mistake.

What if the call is to inform you that you did not get the job? It's a terrible feeling to hear that someone else has been selected instead of you. Sadness, anger and frustration can be but a few of the immediate emotional reactions. So how do you respond? With the same grace as you would when accepting a position. The enthusiasm obviously won't be there, but your professionalism must remain intact. Why? Because time and time again schools find multiple, high-quality candidates for a single position.

Perhaps they were impressed, but didn't feel you were the best fit for that particular position. Maybe they wanted to hire you as well, but another applicant simply edged you out. It's possible the other person had a connection to someone calling the shots and that is why they were selected. Maybe you had a great personality, perfect answers and did everything right, but you just weren't perceived as being experienced enough for the job. Regardless of the reason, if they did like you, they may pass your name on to another school in the district that has an opening or they may want to consider you again the next time that they have a vacancy. It happens all the time, so don't ruin the effort that you've put forth by acting unprofessional or rude. Your journey isn't over yet and burnt bridges will only slow your travel.

Activities and Discussion

Welcome to the activities and discussion section for chapter nine. Everything you need to participate is located on the website that accompanies this book:

www.nelb.info

- In the Chapter Nine Forum "Interview Analysis", tell us what went right and wrong with a recent interview experience. If you don't have any experience yet, feel free to discuss one of your mock interviews.

- How did you word the "Thank You" card to your prospective employer? Share in the Chapter Nine Forum "Thank You Examples".

* In addition to your own thoughts, you are welcome to respond to the posts of other users. Please make sure to protect the private information of others at all times on our website. Use pseudonyms and eliminate any contact information for individuals referenced. Thank you for your cooperation.

Chapter Ten

If All Else Fails

Great Blunders In Job Search History

Forgetting to carry the one, costs Albert
yet another job.

The frustration of not being able to find a job in education can be overwhelming. I should know. I lived it for two years. Coming fresh out of college as a cocky and brash young man with a degree I was sure that I would be hired to a position in one of my desired districts. I had already applied to my high school alma mater as well as several of the surrounding districts that I held in high regard.

As the summer began and I had yet to be contacted, I became frustrated with the situation. If I was unwanted by my choice schools then I was ready to blow off the whole state. I completed numerous out of state applications (with little regard for where I was actually qualified) and sat back, waiting for the interview requests to roll in. They didn't.

I spent that first year out of college working as a used car salesman. I vented my frustration to whoever would listen for a solid six months before realizing that I may be the one to blame. In the evenings I began structuring a new plan of attack. Through some research and inquiry I came to realize that my resume needed scrapped and my targeted districts had to be reconsidered.

I sent my newly polished work out to a different batch of employers. This time I sent it to many more employers. They were districts that were in need of services that I could offer (and services that I was certified to perform).

The days crept by. I finally had opportunities at two separate interviews, both of which went poorly. I was sunk. Before I knew it, another school year was starting without me.

It was time for a decision. I could drag myself back to the used car lot and continue with a job I hated or dig down and commit myself to getting a job over the course of the next year. I chose the latter. I swallowed my pride and sought out a job as a paraprofessional. A local district that was not one of my desired employers interviewed me and decided to take a chance.

At first it was depressing, but then a funny thing happened. For the first time in my entire life, I shut up, worked hard and listened instead of running my mouth. Although I perceived that my instructional abilities were superior to the teachers around me, I kept this to myself. I volunteered for every opportunity that I could find. I took classes to continue my education in the evening and I showed respect to all of my peers. I cared for every student I came in contact with and made sure that they knew I was there to make a difference in their lives. In a word, I changed.

My prospects changed as well. When I sent out my resume in the spring I had authentic experience in the classroom (not just student teaching), a new degree I was working towards and references that gave me glowing recommendations. Calls for interviews came in and this time I was prepared. My answers were spot on. My enthusiasm, knowledge, and willingness to be a part of a team were on display.

I was hired as a classroom teacher before the summer had even arrived.

I loved my new job. I loved the students, the faculty I worked with and the fact that I didn't have to try to sell overpriced automobiles to unsuspecting customers. I loved my new way of life.

Since then I've moved through several more jobs and I've enjoyed each in its own unique way. I learned a valuable lesson over the course of those two years though. The opportunities are out there, but you have to go get them. They aren't going to come to you. Much like life, the job search meets no one half way.

~ Calvin, Principal

Chapter Ten: If All Else Fails
What To Do If The School Year Begins Without You

"I can't believe that we drove around all day and there's not a single job in this town. There is nothing, nada, zip!"

"Yeah! Unless you wanna work forty hours a week!"
~ Harry to Lloyd, Dumb and Dumber

It's August. New bulletin boards are on the walls, lessons are planned, school supplies are flying off the shelves and the back to school buzz is in the air. The only problem is that you aren't a part of that buzz. You haven't been hired for a job.

If the school year has indeed started without you, rest assured that it is not the end of the world. You are not alone in this situation and it is important to keep some perspective. Get out of the front row and climb into the balcony to take a look at the big picture. This is *one* year.

One year is a small time frame in the course of a career, but that doesn't mean that you shouldn't make the most of the opportunity. You have to choose how you are going to approach it. Are you going to wallow in self pity about not being hired or are you going to make an investment in bettering yourself over the course of the year so the outcome is different next time? Some questions to consider are:

- Where can you work this year (as a substitute, paraprofessional, etc.) to improve your chances for the next round of hiring?
- If you work as a substitute, paraprofessional, in the after school program or as a volunteer how can you be memorable to those that you work with? How can you be the best colleague they've ever worked with?
- With whom can you network?
- Should you do something to further your education during the course of the year?
- How else can you get your foot in the door?
- What can you do to strengthen your resume before next year?
- Did you limit yourself too much on location/positions in your job hunt?
- Do you need to improve your public speaking by finding opportunities to practice in front of a group?
- Are there other grades, subjects, schools or districts that you could consider?

With a little careful planning and forethought, the start of next school year can look completely different.

Conclusion

*"Nobody can go back and start a new beginning, but anyone
can start today and make a new ending."*
~ *Maria Robinson*

This section brings the main portion of our book to a close. There is certainly no guarantee as to what your career has in store for you (particularly given the unstable job market of today). However, by practicing the techniques within this book your likelihood of being hired will improve dramatically. Something should be learned with every attempt to obtain a job (whether hired or not). It is a continuous cycle of improvement if approached with open eyes and a willingness to learn.

The pages that follow are an appendix that will provide you with additional tips, cover letters, resumes and interview questions. Additionally, you can find a wealth of additional information at our website:

www.nelb.info

- or you can contact us with questions at -

nelbbook@gmail.com

We wish you the best of luck on your upcoming journey. There are work and obstacles ahead, but if you persevere you can emerge victorious. As you travel this difficult road, remember to keep an eye out for your colleagues. Together we can work to make sure that no educator is left behind.

Activities and Discussion

Welcome to the activities and discussion section for chapter ten. Everything you need to participate is located on the website that accompanies this book:

www.nelb.info

- The job search is a difficult process that can be very stressful. Exercising, dinner with friends, games and good movies are just some of the ways that we like to unwind. How do you relax and keep yourself fresh? Share your thoughts in the Chapter Ten Forum "Recipe for Relaxation".

- You know what your resume looks like now, but what do you want it to look like in the future? Draft a copy of your "future resume." What are you going to accomplish prior to next year that you will be able to add? Write these items in a different color, print out your future resume and use it as motivation each day. You can also share it in the Chapter Ten Forum thread called "Future Resumes".

- What wasn't covered in our book that you still have questions about? Post to the Chapter Ten Forum thread "Lingering Questions" so we can help you with any unresolved concerns.

* In addition to your own thoughts, you are welcome to respond to the posts of other users. Please make sure to protect the private information of others at all times on our website. Use pseudonyms and eliminate any contact information for individuals referenced. Thank you for your cooperation.

Appendix

Supplementary Materials

Great Blunders In Job Search History

It was at that moment that Neil realized his resume
editing should have been a bit more thorough.

Top Ten Rules of the Job Search

1. Be open-minded. If you limit yourself to specific jobs and locations then you eliminate a world of possibilities.

2. Outwork the competition. If you do your current job better than others, then employers will come to realize you are likely to excel at your future job as well.

3. Do your homework. Research potential jobs better than your peers and you will outperform them during the interview.

4. Over prepare. By practicing sample questions and mock interviews you will be more comfortable with the real thing.

5. Edit your applications, cover letters and resumes to perfection. Make them flawless and specific to your needs.

6. Never stop improving. How have you improved, how are you improving and how will you continue to improve in the future?

7. Network continuously and remember to ask specific questions. Put your connections to work.

8. Be optimistic and create a positive image for yourself. Leave others no choice but to like you. The right image will earn you positive references.

9. Give specific answers to interview questions. Generalities are unmemorable and unmemorable people will remain unemployed.

10. Remain vigilant. The job search can be a grueling process. Stay strong and emerge victorious.

Additional Analyzed Cover Letters

This section contains three sample cover letters from experienced teachers. Each cover letter is displayed in its original format and is then critiqued. The first one is poorly done, the second is mediocre and the third is a model cover letter.

Many readers will want more guidance than three sample cover letters can provide. For additional assistance, there are more analyzed cover letters in chapter four of this book as well as numerous model cover letters on our website at www.nelb.info.

9 May 2011

Mellville ISD
194 North Main
Anywhere, TX 67449
Attention: James Seamore, Superintendent

RE: 6-12th Grade School Principal Assignment within Melville Middle & High School.

I was very pleased to hear about the opening of the High School Principal Assignment within Melville Middle & High School. My resume and application are attached for your review. It is my desire work in a district that has an appreciation of lifelong learning and will be a contributing participant in a changing world. I am a highly motivated, team oriented leader, ready to lead, direct, and administer all school operations and activities of a middle and high school community. Through my experiences and roles in administration and teaching I have implemented instructional programs, supported services, and directed facility and ground operations. I have also coordinated all aspects of building maintenance, student activities, and community relations. I value the importance of community and will collaborate with the school's community as your school principal. It is my objective to be a team member with the district administrative team, the building staff, parents and students of Melville Middle & Melville High School. Recently, I worked in the Central Lane School District as their Assistant Principal / Athletic and Activities Director within Central Lane Junior & Senior High School.

A leader is one who transforms a good school into a great school through personal humility, hard work, teamwork, dedication, holding to your ethics and professional will. Everyday I strive to form a building that cultivates a learning community, engages students in their education, and maintains student discipline, while at the same time working as a community with staff and students to achieve the district and state vision of learning.

An administrator's role is to help remove obstacles and support teachers so student academic and behavioral success can occur in the classroom. My goal is to use a team-oriented approach to establish and maintain an emotionally healthy and safe school climate that allows students and teachers to focus on learning. My strengths and experiences support my ability to achieve positive success in leading a building to realize this environment. I am flexible, honest, professional, budget conscious, and sympathetic to students needs. I can honestly and effectively communicate with staff, parents, students, community members and local businesses. As a leader, I make decisions in the best interest of the students, work to meet required state-wide and district outcomes, communicate with and report to interested parties in a timely manner, stay current on educational developments like Project based curriculum, Proficiency Based Instruction, 90 / 90 / 90 schools, best practice research, hire and retain highly qualified staff, specialize in middle to high school transitions, and finally student safety and security within a school building.

One of my major strengths is consistent student discipline. As an administrator, I feel it is important adhere to building and district policy and support teachers and students by creating a safe, enjoyable working environment. Through my experiences and using the Positive Behavior Support Program with staff involvement and buy in as a team we have been able to reduce the overall amount of building referrals from 862 student referrals to 435 student referrals within a three year period. Having students learn they must be responsible and accountable for their behaviors and thinking outside of the box with consequences has reduced discipline within the classroom and on campus. If common expectations are taught and enforced with students, then teachers can concentrate on motivating and teaching. Careful attention to procedures and student's rights, using due process, assures consistency in discipline for each student. My goal in student behavior management is to create responsible, respectful, and trustworthy citizens for the future.

A second major strength is organization. As an administrator it is vital to know what is going on in your school and have easy access to needed resources and materials. Having an organized schedule allows an administrator

Cover Letter #4 Gary Binter (continued)

to have a visible presence in the hallways every morning and after school, during lunch, between classes, during recess, school functions, and most important in the classroom. Being organized also facilitates communication and interactions with others.

I will establish an open door policy with my leadership team, building staff, students, parents and maintain continuous two-way communication. Through flowing communication I am able to ensure a better understanding of school programs, activities, goals, objectives, and school and community needs and desires.

Throughout my career in education my experiences as an administrator, college instructor, building specialist, classroom teacher, leadership advisor, and athletic coach, have been diverse, challenging, and broad in scope. I have been the liaison for several Parent Organizations, written student and coaching handbooks, and been a member of several committees including Site Council, CARE Team, Safety Committee, and the Athletic Review Board. I have collected, analyzed, and reviewed data for building-wide Annual Yearly Progress, student achievement, and athletic eligibility. I have created and developed school master schedules, assisted with TAG testing, helped implement a positive behavior program called Positive Behavior Support (PBS), supported a successful all-day kindergarten literacy program called CHIPS, participated in curriculum adoption K-12 multipliable subject areas, obtained my CERT (Community Emergency Response Team) certification, and mentored and evaluated staff. I have successfully worked with a classroom of students as a Kindergarten teacher. I have also had an opportunity to work in a bilingual building (with two special needs classes, a DLC and SCIP) as the Physical Education Specialist. Most importantly, I have learned to understand the needs of diverse students and the support and resources teachers require in helping them be successful.

Given the opportunity to lead, I will work diligently with staff on positive relations while at the same time creating and fostering a building tone that inspires and encourages staff and students to achieve success. Working cooperatively as a team to develop proficiency based Instruction, a continued focused on state standards, and looking for opportunities to expand student and staff capabilities. By approaching education as a partnership of students, staff, parents, and community we will all grow and develop. My resume and application packet detail the rest of my skills and qualifications. My experiences and insight can be utilized to the advantage of your administration team and school community. I work meticulously to achieve results and look forward to discussing how I can contribute to the Melville Independent School District's future success. In the interim, thank you for your consideration and attention.

Sincerely,

Gary Binter

Gary Binter, MPEAA
3885 West Ct NE
Anywhere, Texas 55505
(555) 555-1623 Home
(555) 555-5116 Cell
Garybinter@email.net
ENC

Analysis of Cover Letter #4, Gary Binter

WARNING: Prolonged exposure to this material is extremely dangerous. Please avoid reading this at all costs. Actual reading of this cover letter could be hazardous to your health.

Sorry, that message was supposed to go *before* the cover letter. If anyone was actually brave enough to suffer through the entire document then we will fully understand if you need to go pour yourself an adult beverage before continuing. Please resist the urge to have a cat scratch your eyes out. We promise that the cover letters get less painful from here.

As for our friend Mr. Binter… Where shall we start? The fact that we're staring at a two page cover letter is probably the most obvious place. What could he have been thinking when making this choice? We know that everything is supposed to be bigger in Texas, but this is excessive. Never, ever, under any circumstances have a cover letter that is longer than one page. It is unnecessary and inexcusable. To top off this lengthy mistake, it is quite obvious that the margins on the page have been modified to the point that they are nearly eliminated. Was Mr. Binter afraid that he might run out of room and need a *third* page? Hard to tell, but with that being said, let's delve further into this abomination and see what we can find. The body of the letter starts off with:

> I was very pleased to hear about the opening of the High School Principal Assignment within Melville Middle & High School. My resume and application are attached for your review. It is my desire work in a district that has an appreciation of lifelong learning and will be a contributing participant in a changing world. I am a highly motivated, team oriented leader, ready to lead, direct, and administer all school operations and activities of a middle and high school community. Through my experiences and roles in administration and teaching I have implemented instructional programs, supported services, and directed facility and ground operations. I have also coordinated all aspects of building maintenance, student activities, and community relations. I value the importance of community and will collaborate with the school's community as your school principal. It is my objective to be a team member with the district administrative team, the building staff, parents and students of Melville Middle & Melville High School. Recently, I worked in the Central Lane School District as their Assistant Principal / Athletic and Activities Director within Central Lane Junior & Senior High School.

This is simply awful. The minor issue is that some basic editing was overlooked:

- "High School Principal Assignment"; why is the "A" capitalized?
- "It is my desire work in a district…"; the word "to" would help out immensely.

These basic points are trivial compared to the main problem though. *The writing is awful.* It has no flow, the organization is minimal and the points are…pointless.

"It is my main objective to be a team member with the district administrative team..." *As opposed to what? Being a team opponent?* Mr. Binter's statement doesn't even make sense. The closing sentence on this paragraph seems as if it were tacked on at random. Actually, that's an apt description of the document as a whole. It's as if individual sentences were arranged based on some warped version of Pin The Tail On The Donkey. Get out the blindfold, spin around a few times, and then tack the sentences on wherever they will stick. On to paragraph two:

> A leader is one who transforms a good school into a great school through personal humility, hard work, teamwork, dedication, holding to your ethics and professional will. Everyday I strive to form a building that cultivates a learning community, engages students in their education, and maintains student discipline, while at the same time working as a community with staff and students to achieve the district and state vision of learning.

In a word: baffling. Why in the world is this here? Why didn't Mr. Binter include definitions for other words? To define "leader" is nice, but it would have been fun to see the meanings of other words as well.

Hippopotamus: A large mammal that lives in the lakes and rivers of Africa, hippopotamuses have hairless bodies and short legs. They are herbivores and can stay under water for long periods of time.

The hippo definition would have been even more ridiculous, but infinitely more entertaining. Regardless of which position is being applied for, it should not be defined in the cover letter. Perceptions of what the job truly "is" can be discussed during an interview. Cover letters are an opportunity to sell yourself and Mr. Binter is doing a lousy job of it. Moving on:

> An administrator's role is to help remove obstacles and support teachers so student academic and behavioral success can occur in the classroom. My goal is to use a team-oriented approach to establish and maintain an emotionally healthy and safe school climate that allows students and teachers to focus on learning. My strengths and experiences support my ability to achieve positive success in leading a building to realize this environment. I am flexible, honest, professional, budget conscious, and sympathetic to students needs. I can honestly and effectively communicate with staff, parents, students, community members and local businesses. As a leader, I make decisions in the best interest of the students, work to meet required state-wide and district outcomes, communicate with and report to interested parties in a timely manner, stay current on educational developments like Project based curriculum, Proficiency Based Instruction, 90 / 90 / 90 schools, best practice research, hire and retain highly qualified staff, specialize in middle to high school transitions, and finally student safety and security within a school building.

Eliminating run on sentences can be a difficult task for first graders. Apparently in some cases it can prove challenging for administrators as well. The final sentence from this paragraph was nearly one hundred words long. *One hundred.* We had a couple of chapters in this book that weren't much longer than that. Up next we find:

> One of my major strengths is consistent student discipline. As an administrator, I feel it is important adhere to building and district policy and support teachers and students by creating a safe, enjoyable working environment. Through my experiences and using the Positive Behavior Support Program with staff involvement and buy in as a team we have been able to reduce the overall amount of building referrals from 862 student referrals to 435 student referrals within a three year period. Having students learn they must be responsible and accountable for their behaviors and thinking outside of the box with consequences has reduced discipline within the classroom and on campus. If common expectations are taught and enforced with students, then teachers can concentrate on motivating and teaching. Careful attention to procedures and student's rights, using due process, assures consistency in discipline for each student. My goal in student behavior management is to create responsible, respectful, and trustworthy citizens for the future.

"Careful attention to procedures and student's rights, using due process, assures consistency in discipline for each student." *"Student's"*, huh? Just one? Apostrophes can be difficult to get the hang of and people misuse them constantly. Don't let this mistake make you appear foolish on a cover letter. If Mr. Binter only cares about one child, then he correctly used "student's rights". If he cares about them all (or even more than one), it should be "students' rights". Let's take some mercy on this ill conceived catastrophe and skip forward:

> Throughout my career in education my experiences as an administrator, college instructor, building specialist, classroom teacher, leadership advisor, and athletic coach, have been diverse, challenging, and broad in scope. I have been the liaison for several Parent Organizations, written student and coaching handbooks, and been a member of several committees including Site Council, CARE Team, Safety Committee, and the Athletic Review Board. I have collected, analyzed, and reviewed data for building-wide Annual Yearly Progress, student achievement, and athletic eligibility. I have created and developed school master schedules, assisted with TAG testing, helped implement a positive behavior program called Positive Behavior Support (PBS), supported a successful all-day kindergarten literacy program called CHIPS, participated in curriculum adoption K-12 multipliable subject areas, obtained my CERT (Community Emergency Response Team) certification, and mentored and evaluated staff. I have successfully worked with a classroom of students as a Kindergarten teacher. I have also had an opportunity to work in a bilingual building (with two special needs classes, a DLC and SCIP) as the Physical Education Specialist. Most importantly, I have learned to understand the needs of diverse students and the support and resources teachers require in helping them be successful.

"Throughout my career in education....have been diverse, challenging, and broad in scope." That's odd. Those characteristics also sum up this cover letter quite well. Mr. Binter treats us to another fifty plus word bomb of a sentence in the middle of this paragraph. Run for cover. He then closes with:

Sincerely,

Gary Binter

Gary Binter, MPEAA
3885 West Ct NE
Anywhere, Texas 55505
(555) 555-1623 Home
(555) 555-5116 Cell
Garybinter@email.net
ENC

There are two mysteries here:

- The first is why Mr. Binter chose to list his name twice. Apparently he decided that once was insufficient.

- The second is Mr. Binter's title of MPEAA. It looks fancy, but we have no clue what it means. A search of the Internet provides only that it is an acronym for the Motion Picture Export Association of America. We're going to assume that this is not what Mr. Binter intended. Of course, who knows? Maybe he's banking on his expertise in selling DVD's of eighties action movies to China.

February 8, 2011

To Whom It May Concern:

I am writing today to apply for a position as a high school English teacher. I have a bachelor's degree from Northern University and am currently working on a master's degree in Curriculum and Instruction.

I taught English for four years at Madison High School in Anywhere, Virginia. While there I was an instructor for both freshmen and sophomore English students. I have worked with students with a wide range of needs and abilities.

Thank you for considering me for this position. Please feel free to contact me at your convenience.

Rich Graham
5551 N. Broadview
Anywhere, Virginia 55558
(555) 555-0068
rgraham@email.com

Analysis of Cover Letter #5, Rich Graham

Here we find a very middle of the road cover letter from Mr. Graham. It is the perfect example of how a cover letter can be structurally correct, yet fail to impress at the same time. Let's look at the opening:

> To Whom It May Concern:
>
> I am writing today to apply for a position as a high school English teacher. I have a bachelor's degree from Northern University and am currently working on a master's degree in Curriculum and Instruction.

No specific person was identified and we are left with a generic, "To Whom It May Concern." Not a deal breaker, but why not invest the small amount of work necessary to identify the correct person? The applicant's work towards a master's degree is certainly a plus. Next Mr. Graham shares his experience:

> I taught English for four years at Madison High School in Anywhere, Virginia. While there I was an instructor for both freshmen and sophomore English students. I have worked with students with a wide range of needs and abilities.

Four years of experience is a respectable length of time for one location. It lets us know that Mr. Graham received tenure at his previous school, so he is likely leaving that job and searching for a new one under his own accord (he probably wasn't non-renewed unless it was due to budget cuts or other issues).

What else did Mr. Graham accomplish in his four years at Madison High? Hopefully his resume contains more specifics because this paragraph about his experience was extremely vague. The cover letter then reaches its closing:

> Thank you for considering me for this position. Please feel free to contact me at your convenience.

Mr. Graham did not have any typos, unnecessary information or serious issues in his cover letter. He also didn't have anything that will overly impress potential employers.

Brevity is good and there is nothing wrong with a short cover letter (it trumps a long one nearly every time) but Mr. Graham may have taken it a step too far. This appears in all likelihood to be a form letter. There are no specifics in it and nothing that would need to be changed before Mr. Graham could send it to numerous employers simultaneously. Perhaps he sent it out through one of the mass application systems that were discussed in chapter three (and later in this appendix).

Overall this is a functional cover letter. It does not eliminate Mr. Graham from contention or make him a leading candidate. It sets the stage for his resume and that is the extent of its usefulness.

Bill Edwards
7500 East 20th Court
Anywhere, NE 55526
(555) 555-6451

January 22, 2011

Mr. Earl Charles
Assistant Superintendent for Human Resources
West Public Schools
500 N. 1st
Anywhere, NE 67202

Dear Mr. Charles:

It is with great interest that I apply for the job of Elementary Assistant Principal for West Public Schools. I believe that both my experience and skills are a perfect match for this position and I would appreciate consideration of my credentials as presented below and in my attached resume. I would bring to this position:

- six years of experience in education, three of which were spent as the lead teacher in my building;

- a demonstrated record of teaching excellence, as shown by meeting the state's standard of excellence guidelines;

- a willingness to work closely with parents, teachers, and community leaders.

I have completed my Master's Degree in Educational Administration and have secured a PK-12 Building Leadership License. I am currently working on an ESOL endorsement. With my education and experience I feel I am well prepared for the wide variety of responsibilities that this job may entail.

I have thoroughly enjoyed my experiences with West Public Schools and would appreciate the opportunity to meet and discuss my qualifications. Thank you for your consideration and I look forward to hearing from you soon.

Sincerely,

Bill Edwards

attachment: resume

Analysis of Cover Letter #6, Bill Edwards

Mr. Edwards has a well polished cover letter. It is free of typos and well structured. Let's take a look at the opening section:

> Dear Mr. Charles:
>
> It is with great interest that I apply for the job of Elementary Assistant Principal for West Public Schools. I believe that both my experience and skills are a perfect match for this position and I would appreciate consideration of my credentials as presented below and in my attached resume. I would bring to this position:

The research was done to make sure this letter was addressed to the correct person. The personalization is a nice touch. There doesn't appear to be much else in the way of individualized details in this letter explaining why Mr. Edwards would be a good match for a specific school's need, but that appears to be because this is an open application for all of the schools in the district. Individual schools that are spread across a district often have vastly varying needs, so the lack of specifics in that regards seems appropriate here. The bullets come next:

> - six years of experience in education, three of which were spent as the lead teacher in my building;
>
> - a demonstrated record of teaching excellence, as shown by meeting the state's standard of excellence guidelines;
>
> - a willingness to work closely with parents, teachers, and community leaders.

This section is quick and easy to read. The bullets add a nice balance of white space to the document, although the third one is somewhat questionable. The initial two bullets both provide justification as to the rationale for the claim. The third one, however, seems to be an opinion. Support for the claim (such as membership on the school's PTO, Site Council, etc.) should have been included, even if there is greater detail to accompany it in the resume. If there is no support that can be added, then the third bullet should have been omitted. The next paragraph discusses education:

> I have completed my Master's Degree in Educational Administration and have secured a PK-12 Building Leadership License. I am currently working on an ESOL endorsement. With my education and experience I feel I am well prepared for the wide variety of responsibilities that this job may entail.

This section shows that the applicant is still working to further his education. Mr. Edwards wasn't satisfied with the minimum requirements alone and is working toward a new certificate. He continues to increase his knowledge while expanding the breadth of his credentials as well. Lifelong learning is an important quality to employers; no one wants to hire someone who is comfortable with the status quo. The cover letter then draws to a close:

I have thoroughly enjoyed my experiences with West Public Schools and would appreciate the opportunity to meet and discuss my qualifications. Thank you for your consideration and I look forward to hearing from you soon.

Sincerely,

Bill Edwards

attachment: resume

There are no issues here. The line "attachment: resume" is fairly common, but it serves no purpose. It is assumed that the resume is attached. Take it or leave it, there is no real need to close with the statement.

Overall this was a very solid cover letter. If Mr. Charles clears up the third bullet then it would improve both the cover letter and his odds of receiving an interview.

Additional Analyzed Resumes

What follows are three sample resumes from experienced teachers. One is poor, one is mediocre and one is a model resume. These are based on real resumes that were submitted to school districts (the names and locations have been changed). Each resume is displayed in its original format and is then analyzed and critiqued by the use of our Resume Rubric. The rubric will help demonstrate which resumes will end up in the trash, which will be considered and which will result in an interview.

To provide additional assistance to you there are three more analyzed resumes in chapter five. There are also numerous examples of model resumes available on our website at www.nelb.info.

Respect
Respect

Jerry B. Bailey
1119 S. Hickory
Anywhere, Ny 55567
(555)555-5756
jerry.bailey@email.com

Respons
Responsibility
Responsibility
Responsibility

Respect
Respect

- Date of birth: August 22, 1986
- Marital Status: Married February 2009
- Family: One child born in 2010
- Health: Excellent
- Current Employer: Central School District, New York Public Schools
- Credentials: City University

Objective
To obtain a K-6 Teaching position in which I can educate students in a positive and supportive environment, based on current curriculum through state standards and differentiated instruction.

Education
-   City University- Anywhere, Ny Campus. Graduated in August 2011.
-   East Community College- Anywhere, Ca. January 2007- December 2008.
-   Mount Adams College- Anywhere, Ca. September 2006- December 2006.
-   South High School- Anywhere, Ca. September 2002- June 2006.

Course Work
-   Introduction to Teaching
-   Assessment in Today's Classroom

- Fundamentals of School's in a Diverse Society
- Managing the Educational Environment
- The Exceptional Child
- Personal and Community Health
- Elementary Student Teaching

Experience
- Teacher, 3rd Grade, West Elementary, Anywhere, NY 2010-2011
- Member of South High School football team 2002-2006
- Member of East Community College football team 2007-2008
- Member of City University football team 2009-2010
- South High School Honor Roll 2002-2006
- Who's Who Among American High School Students 2006.
- South High School freshmen football coach 2006.
- Volunteer Little League baseball coach
- 09'-11' Shoulder Pads and Paragraphs (volunteer reading to kindergarten classes)
- City University football youth day (2009-2010).
- New York Kids Fitness Day (City University, 2009-2010).
- Secondary student teaching (West Middle School, Anywhere, Ny).
- Elementary student teaching (Lincoln Elementary School, Anywhere, Ny).

Computer Skills
- Microsoft Word
- Microsoft PowerPoint

References

- Andi Hayes, City University Assistant Professor/Division Chair, Education
  andi.hayes@email.edu Phone: (555) 555-5200 Ext. 5076
- Allison Belcher, City University Assistant Professor, Physical Education/HPER Chair
  allison.belcher@email.edu Phone: (555) 555-5200 Ext. 5417
- Karl Klingsick, City University Head Football Coach
  karl.klingsick@email.edu Phone: (555) 555-5200 Ext. 5419

Analysis of Sample Resume #4, Jerry Bailey

Every once in a while the planets align and a resume comes along that is so bad it achieves the pinnacle of atrociousness. This is one of those resumes. Mr. Bailey has already eliminated himself from contention based on this alone:

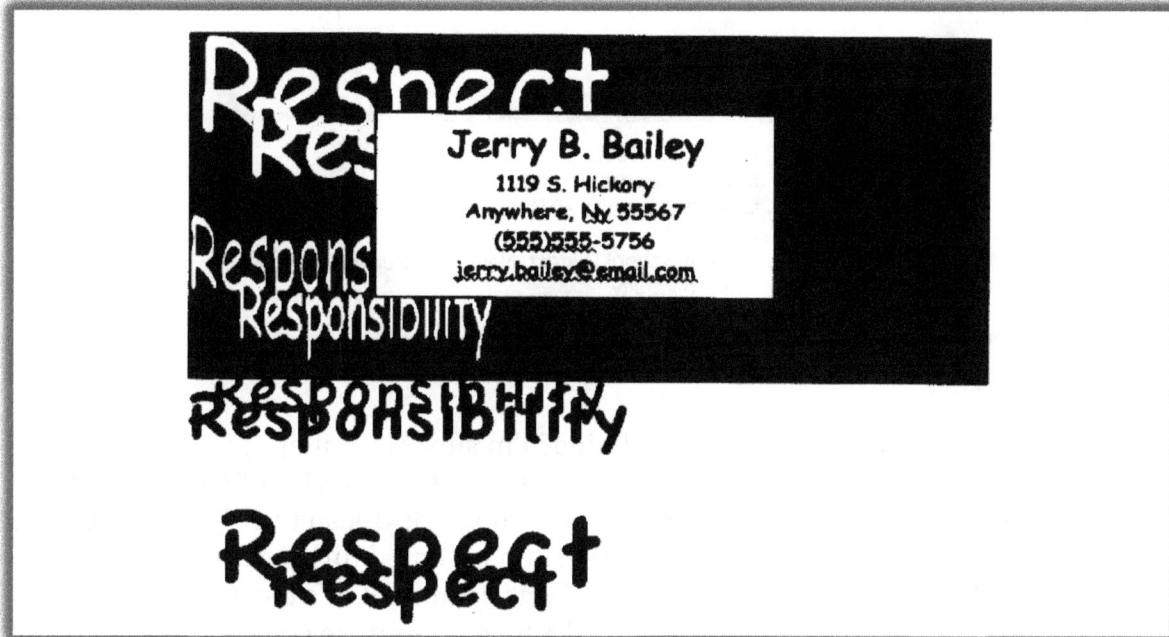

Words cannot describe our initial reaction to this header. It is obvious that Mr. Bailey was attempting to be unique and he has certainly accomplished that. The very notion that he honestly saw this as a good idea speaks volumes of his decision-making capabilities. This is not a candidate that is going to be viewed as hirable by any sensible person. We even attempted our own rendition of the work that showed what was seen through an employer's eyes:

There's a difference between originality and ineptitude. We can make the distinction between a Jackson Pollock and someone who spilled a bucket of paint on a canvas. This resembles the latter. The two rectangles containing Mr. Bailey's personal information would have been an acceptable touch. The wild display of "Respect" and "Responsibility" stretching halfway down the page never should have made the final cut. Next we find a bizarre section containing personal background information:

```
- Date of birth:      August 22, 1986
- Marital Status:     Married February 2009
- Family:             One child born in 2010
- Health:             Excellent
- Current Employer:   Central School District, New York Public Schools
- Credentials:        City University
```

Why, oh why, was this ever included? I'm sure Mr. Bailey is a proud father, but his child should not be on the resume. His health is "excellent"? Kind of makes you wonder if a recent physical is attached to the back, doesn't it? Then there's the alignment. Why are the hyphens in this section indented further than the hyphens in the rest of the resume? As with much of this document, it's hard to tell. Regardless, we had so much fun revising the header, that we couldn't resist modifying this portion as well:

```
- Date of birth:      August 22, 1986
- Marital Status:     Married February 2009
- Family:             One child. I also have a mother and a father!
- Health:             Physically Excellent, Mentally Questionable
- Current Employer:   Currently Undergoing a Nonrenewal
- Credentials:        City University
- Blood Type:         B Positive
- Listening To:       80's Punk Rock and Kenny G
- Likes:              Long Walks on the Beach
- Dislikes:           Mean People
- Paper or Plastic:   Definitely Plastic
```

It may not be an improvement, but it's definitely just as pointless. Let's move on to the body of the resume. We're struggling to adequately express our thoughts, because we can't help but focus on all of the hyphens on the left side of the page. They're everywhere! It's as if a windstorm tore through and littered the entire page with little tree limbs from top to bottom. If Mr. Bailey had chosen bullets instead of hyphens, the resume would look as if someone had opened fire on it with a machine gun. Something has to be done with this before anything else can be discussed. The easiest solution is to check for any irrelevant information that can be omitted. If we can get rid of some of the entries, then we can eliminate a number of the hyphens as well. Let's go through and see what to dispose of, starting with "Education":

Education
- City University- Anywhere, Ny Campus. Graduated in August 2011.
- East Community College- Anywhere, Ca. January 2007- December 2008.
- Mount Adams College- Anywhere, Ca. September 2006- December 2006.
- South High School- Anywhere, Ca. September 2002- June 2006.

This is a train wreck, plain and simple. Out of these four entries, not one of them belongs in their current form. Employers who take a close look at this section may interpret it as follows:

"It appears that in '05 Mr. Bailey graduated from high school. That's a relief, we wouldn't want to hire a high school drop out as our new teacher. It's a shame he didn't backtrack a little further, I'm quite curious where he attended daycare... Let's see, next he went to Mount Adams College for...four months. Hmmmmm. Well, I'm guessing he had fun majoring in Beer Pong and girls for that short stint and then it looks like mom and dad cut him off so he had to return home for a couple of years at the local community college. Now he is attending another university and expects to graduate soon."

Now this may be a crude and completely unfair interpretation of Mr. Bailey's education. There could have been any number of events in his life that would have triggered his changes in location. Is it fair for an employer to make any of those assumptions? No. Will many of them do so anyway? Yes. So don't give them the opportunity. Mr. Bailey could restructure this section as follows:

Education
Bachelor of Science in Education, Projected Graduation: August 2011
City University, Anywhere, NY

That's it. No high school references and no listings for universities where a degree was not obtained. They aren't relevant and it does not add to the probability of obtaining an interview, so why include them? The only exception would be if the high school/junior college information would grab the employer's attention. One example would be if you are an alumni of the school where you are applying. Those doing the hiring often like the familiarity of a candidate who knows the school or surrounding area. Next we have Mr. Bailey's course work:

```
Course Work
-   Introduction to Teaching
-   Assessment in Today's Classroom
-   Fundamentals of School's in a Diverse Society
-   Managing the Educational Environment
-   The Exceptional Child
-   Personal and Community Health
-   Elementary Student Teaching
```

Whoever told Mr. Bailey that this was a good idea is either clueless or doesn't like him very much. Maybe it was done of his own accord. Regardless, it needs to be eliminated. No one cares about "Intro To Teaching." *Every* teacher has taken Intro To Teaching. Mr. Bailey may as well have written that he has a pulse; it would have impressed the same percentage of potential employers. This section needs to be eliminated in its entirety. It wouldn't be acceptable for someone fresh out of college, much less an individual with a year of teaching under his belt. On top of that, if you look at the original resume you will see that this information started on page one and continued on page two. Never let a section carry from one page to the next on a resume. Let's move on to "Experience":

```
Experience
-   Teacher, 3rd Grade, West Elementary, Anywhere, NY 2010-2011
-   Member of South High School football team 2002-2006
-   Member of East Community College football team 2007-2008
-   Member of City University football team 2009-2010
-   South High School Honor Roll 2002-2006
-   Who's Who Among American High School Students 2006.
-   South High School freshmen football coach 2006.
-   Volunteer Little League baseball coach
-   09'-11' Shoulder Pads and Paragraphs (volunteer reading to kindergarten
    classes)
-   City University football youth day (2009-2010).
-   New York Kids Fitness Day (City University, 2009-2010).
-   Secondary student teaching (West Middle School, Anywhere, Ny).
-   Elementary student teaching (Lincoln Elementary School, Anywhere, Ny).
```

The most glaring issue here is that Mr. Bailey gives one brief line to his actual teaching experience from last year. We're going to go out on a limb and make an assumption that the school year might not have gone so well for him, but actual teaching experience is *still* the most powerful thing he has listed. Only briefly pointing it out makes it appear as if he is trying to hide something (which he very well may be).

Another flaw with this section is the organization. Resumes should always have dates listed in order. They can either be arranged from the most recent date going backwards or vice versa, but order is necessary. This random jumble of dates is both confusing and unappealing.

Aside from these issues, there is some authentic experience in this section that could help the candidate out, but there are also some items that need eliminated, such as:

- "South High School Honor Roll": It undoubtedly takes commitment for anyone to achieve honor roll status at their high school. That hard work will pay off when working to be admitted to college. However, it does nothing for an applicant's prospects of landing a teaching job. High school has come and gone; it's time to move on. This needs to be taken off the list.

- "Who's Who Among American High School Students": We're not going to state our personal opinions on the credibility of this distinction, but type it into a search engine and see what you get. Lots of different sites with references to it being a scam, right? Many college admissions offices and employers will look at this and conclude, *"Oh, he was foolish enough to spend money to obtain recognition for this 'honor'."* This (and any other questionable recognitions) need to be eliminated from all resumes.

- "City University football youth day": Why only two of the five words were capitalized is beyond us, but it doesn't matter because this either needs modified or eliminated. Unless Mr. Bailey organized the event, doing an activity for one day is not resume worthy. It's a nice gesture and hopefully a nice memory, but that's it. Volunteering somewhere on a regular basis shows character. Volunteering somewhere for a few hours is great, but not something that will get you a job.

- "New York Kids Fitness Day": All of the above points from "City University football youth day" are applicable here, as well as the fact that if Mr. Bailey does insist on using this, he should at least put the apostrophe in "Kids' Day".

- The numerous athletic references could certainly be reduced (if you played college football, we can make the logical assumption that you played high school football as well) but are only necessary if Mr. Bailey is attempting to acquire a coaching position.

Next we find the separate heading "Computer Skills" along with two hyphenated items:

Computer Skills
- Microsoft Word
- Microsoft PowerPoint

Microsoft Word and PowerPoint, huh? Well congratulations, you're qualified to be a third grader. Word and PowerPoint are not what we are looking for when we're talking about tech savvy. In this day and age there are some things that are assumed. Familiarity with a word processor ranks right up there with the ability to turn on a light switch. The resume concludes with the "References" section:

References

- Andi Hayes, City University Assistant Professor/Division Chair, Education
andi.hayes@email.edu Phone: (555) 555-5200 Ext. 5076
- Allison Belcher, City University Assistant Professor, Physical Education/HPER
Chair
allison.belcher@email.edu Phone: (555) 555-5200 Ext. 5417
- Karl Klingsick, City University Head Football Coach
karl.klingsick@email.edu Phone: (555) 555-5200 Ext. 5419

We're positive that Mr. Bailey had some logical reason for listing his references in this fashion. We simply can't fathom what that logic was. A little white space would have gone a long way. One line between each of the references to give them their own individual spot would help immensely. Not only that, but since the three distinct references would be immediately recognizable the hyphens could be deleted. There is no mention of supervisors from his teaching job, which only adds to the suspicions we alluded to earlier.

Once the resume is gutted of the above mentioned items then we can start over and try again with what is left. By elaborating on what is really important, leaving some white space and sparing the hyphen key on his keyboard from any further abuse, Mr. Bailey can dramatically improve this document and his chances of landing an interview. Let's take a look at how this one scores on the resume rubric.

No Educator Left Behind
Resume Rubric

	Fail	Pass
Format	Formatting (font size, font type, punctuation, capitalization, bullets, etc.) is inconsistent	Formatting (font size, font type, punctuation, capitalization, bullets, etc.) is consistent
	Not all mandatory headings (Education, Experience, References) are represented	All mandatory headings (Education, Experience, References) are represented
	White space is inadequate or excessive	White space is appropriate
Education	Education does not meet requirements	Education meets requirements
	Dates are not in a logical order	Dates are in a logical order
	Certifications are not listed	Certifications are listed
Experience	Experience does not meet requirements	Experience does meet requirements
	Dates are not in a logical order	Dates are in a logical order
	Job duties are general and/or irrelevant	Job duties are specific and relevant
Editing	Typographical and/or grammatical errors are present (confirmed by multiple editors)	No typographical and/or grammatical errors are present (confirmed by multiple editors)
	Inaccurate and/or false information	No inaccurate and/or false information
Wording	Weak and/or unprofessional vocabulary	Strong and/or professional vocabulary
	Inconsistent tenses	Consistent Tenses
	Wording is confusing and difficult to read	Wording is clear and easy to read
	An excessive amount of jargon is present	Jargon is not excessive
	Unnecessary information is present	Unnecessary information has been removed
Length	Inappropriate length (three pages or more, plus references)	Appropriate length (one or two pages plus references)
References	References are not listed	References are listed
	References are not listed in a consistent format (name, title, contact information)	References are listed consistently (name, title, contact information)
	No supervisors are listed	Supervisors are listed

__Sample Resume #5, Gerald Douglas__

Gerald Douglas

500 8th Street   (555) 555-0088
Anywhere, Minnesota 55555   gdouglas@email.com

EDUCATION
> **B.S. in Elementary Education,** December 2004
> Central University, Anywhere, MN
> **ESL Certification,** 2007

TEACHING EXPERIENCE
> **Classroom Teacher, Coach,** August 2009-2011
> Clark County Junior High, 6th -8th Grades, Anywhere, MN
> * Developed lesson plans for teaching 6th – 8th grades
> * Effectively used different teaching strategies and methods
> * Coached football, basketball, and baseball at junior high and high school level
>
> **Classroom Teacher / Coach,** August 2005-May 2009
> South Elementary School, Fifth and Sixth Grade, Anywhere, MN

OTHER EXPERIENCE
> **Sales Representative,** June 2011-Present
> Widget Equipment Company, Anywhere, MN
> * Market Widget Equipment
> * Developed customer base
> * Submitted customer lone contracts

QUALIFICATIONS
> * Computer experience in Microsoft Word, PowerPoint, Excel; Internet Explorer,
> * Extensive coaching experience at both Junior High and High School level

RELATED EXPERIENCE
> **Volunteer Little League Baseball Coach,** Recreation Commission, Anywhere, MN
> **Baseball and Softball Umpire,** Recreation Commission, Anywhere, MN

COMMUNITY SERVICE
> * Clark County Volunteer Fire Department and EMS
> * Clark County Amusement Association Volunteer
> * Park and Recreation Board Member and Volunteer

PROFESSIONAL ORGANIZATIONS/ HONORS
> Lamda Lamda Lamda Secretary, Central University 2002-2004
> Minnesota Baseball Coaches Association

REFERENCES
> Available upon request

Analysis of Sample Resume #5, Gerald Douglas

Mr. Douglass has come close to having a quality resume, but has failed to perform the necessary fine-tuning to achieve the desired finished product. Let's examine his teaching experience first:

TEACHING EXPERIENCE
Classroom Teacher, Coach, August 2009-2011
Clark County Junior High, 6th-8th Grades, Anywhere, MN
- Developed lesson plans for teaching 6th – 8th grades
- Effectively used different teaching strategies and methods
- Coached football, basketball, and baseball at junior high and high school level

While there is nothing inaccurate about "Developed lesson plans" and "Effectively used different teaching strategies and methods" they simply don't bring anything additional to the table. There is nothing that an employer will be intrigued by in either of those bullets. They are far too generic and are thus a waste of space. Surely Mr. Douglas has accomplished something in his teaching career that is more brag worthy than those items. Next we find "Other Experience":

OTHER EXPERIENCE
Sales Representative, June 2011-Present
Widget Equipment Company, Anywhere, MN
- Market Widget Equipment
- Developed customer base
- Submitted customer lone contracts

It appears that Mr. Douglas has stepped outside of education and acquired a different job. There's nothing wrong with this, although it would be wise of him to explain the circumstances in his cover letter. The major issue with this section is the word "lone" which was supposed to be "loan." Spell checks won't catch words that are spelled correctly (no matter how out of context they are). The next heading is "Qualifications":

QUALIFICATIONS
- Computer experience in Microsoft Word, PowerPoint, Excel; Internet Explorer,
- Extensive coaching experience at both Junior High and High School level

This section is unnecessary. Mr. Douglas knows how to use the Internet? That's how he plans on separating himself from the competition? If he builds computers or creates his own websites then employers may be enticed, but no one is impressed by an individual who can use the Internet. The vast majority of people have a solid grasp of how to go online.[5] Furthermore, why is there such inconsistent comma use throughout the first bullet? Why was a semicolon used after "Excel;" and why is there a random comma at the end of the line for no apparent reason?

The information presented in the second bullet regarding coaching experience was shared at numerous points throughout the resume. Why bother writing it again? The headings really begin to stack up as we find the third type of experience listed by Mr. Douglas, "Related Experience."

RELATED EXPERIENCE
Volunteer Little League Baseball Coach, Recreation Commission, Anywhere, MN
Baseball and Softball Umpire, Recreation Commission, Anywhere, MN

Where are the bullets for this section? They are mysteriously absent from both here and the "Professional Organizations/Honors" portion of the resume. Bullets aren't the biggest issue though, because Mr. Douglas could have easily listed these items elsewhere. The volunteer coaching belongs with "Community Service" and the umpire work for the recreation commission would have been appropriate in "Other Experience." Let's skip ahead to "Professional Organizations/Honors":

PROFESSIONAL ORGANIZATIONS/ HONORS
Lamda Lamda Lamda Secretary, Central University 2002-2004
Minnesota Baseball Coaches Association

Candidates (especially those fresh out of college) sometimes list responsibilities or memberships in fraternities/sororities on their resumes. We would not recommend this action. The odds of you belonging to the same fraternity or sorority as your potential employer are extremely slim. The only exception would be if you are sure the employer belonged to the same Greek organization as you.

If you did belong to a fraternity or sorority in college it is likely that you were involved in various forms of community service and charitable works. Those are the items to list on your resume. Finally Mr. Douglas concludes with:

```
REFERENCES
Available upon request
```

As mentioned in chapter five, listing your references is the more logical choice. Mr. Douglas should have included them on a second page prior to submitting his credentials.

Overall this is not a bad resume. With a little effort and careful thought it could be quite good. Mr. Douglas overlooked a few issues, prohibiting himself from completing a quality resume and possibly costing himself the opportunity to interview. You can see how this affected his score on our resume rubric on the following page.

	Fail	Pass
Format	Formatting (font size, font type, punctuation, capitalization, bullets, etc.) is inconsistent	Formatting (font size, font type, punctuation, capitalization, bullets, etc.) is consistent
	Not all mandatory headings (Education, Experience, References) are represented	All mandatory headings (Education, Experience, References) are represented
	White space is inadequate or excessive	White space is appropriate
Education	Education does not meet requirements	Education meets requirements
	Dates are not in a logical order	Dates are in a logical order
	Certifications are not listed	Certifications are listed
Experience	Experience does not meet requirements	Experience does meet requirements
	Dates are not in a logical order	Dates are in a logical order
	Job duties are general and/or irrelevant	Job duties are specific and relevant
Editing	Typographical and/or grammatical errors are present (confirmed by multiple editors)	No typographical and/or grammatical errors are present (confirmed by multiple editors)
	Inaccurate and/or false information	No inaccurate and/or false information
Wording	Weak and/or unprofessional vocabulary	Strong and/or professional vocabulary
	Inconsistent tenses	Consistent Tenses
	Wording is confusing and difficult to read	Wording is clear and easy to read
	An excessive amount of jargon is present	Jargon is not excessive
	Unnecessary information is present	Unnecessary information has been removed
Length	Inappropriate length (three pages or more, plus references)	Appropriate length (one or two pages plus references)
References	References are not listed	References are listed
	References are not listed in a consistent format (name, title, contact information)	References are listed consistently (name, title, contact information)
	No supervisors are listed	Supervisors are listed

CINDY DOWNING

OBJECTIVE

To obtain a secondary mathematics position and share my love of learning.

EXPERIENCE

2008–Present	East High School	Anywhere, LA

- Instructor for Algebra and Geometry
- Helped Students Successfully Meet AYP
- Teacher of the Year Nominee, 2009
- Student Improvement Team Member

2003–2008	Washington Middle School	Anywhere, LA

- Instructor for Trigonometry and Algebra
- Helped Students Successfully Meet AYP
- Eighth Grade Boy's Basketball Coach

EDUCATION AND CERTIFICATION

2009	State University	Anywhere, LA

- Master of Science, Curriculum and Instruction

2008	Class A Teaching Certification

2003	Eastern University	Anywhere, SD

- Bachelor of Science, Mathematics
- Bachelor of Science, Secondary Education

COMMUNITY SERVICE

2008–Present	Big Brothers Big Sisters Volunteer
2006–Present	Inner City Youth Basketball Camp Volunteer

CDOWNING@EMAIL.COM
555 WEST AVENUE • ANYWHERE, ALABAMA 55555 • (555) 555-5555

CINDY DOWNING

REFERENCES

Bill Lawrence
Principal, East High School
(555) 555-5000
blawrence@email.com

Sara Johnson
Principal, Washington Middle School
(555) 555-5550
sjohnson@email.com

Ralph Calhoun
Math Teacher, East High School
(555) 555-5050
rcalhoun@email.com

Analysis of Sample Resume #6, Cindy Downing

Here we find a high quality resume from an experienced math teacher. Our only significant issue with this work comes at the beginning in Ms. Downing's heading:

CINDY DOWNING

We did a double take upon originally seeing this. Where is Ms. Downing's contact information? It didn't take us long to spot it at the bottom of the page, but we're still not in favor of this format. Ms. Downing's address, phone number and email address should all be clearly visible under her name. Let's move on to experience:

EXPERIENCE

2008–Present East High School   **Anywhere, LA**
- Instructor for Algebra and Geometry
- Helped Students Successfully Meet AYP
- Teacher of the Year Nominee, 2009
- Site Council Chair
- Student Improvement Team Member

2003–2008   Washington Middle School   **Anywhere, LA**
- Instructor for Trigonometry and Algebra
- Helped Students Successfully Meet AYP
- Eigth Grade Boy's Basketball Coach
- Building Improvement Team Chair
- PTO Member

Ms. Downing has a nice selection of specific duties and accomplishments from each of her positions. With the use of only ten bullets she has demonstrated her leadership and involvement (two chair positions on committees), her willingness to work with parents (PTO), athletic contributions (coaching) and a high level of performance (Teacher of the Year Nominee). The next section covers education:

```
EDUCATION AND CERTIFICATION
                    2009        State University              Anywhere, LA
                    ■ Master of Science, Curriculum and Instruction


                    2008        Class A Teaching Certification


                    2003        Eastern University            Anywhere, SD
                    ■ Bachelor of Science, Mathematics
                    ■ Bachelor of Science, Secondary Education
```

There are no issues present here. Ms. Downing's education is clearly stated and very impressive. Three different degrees makes for a definite attention grabber. "Community Service" is up next:

```
COMMUNITY SERVICE
                2008–Present   Big Brothers Big Sisters Volunteer

                2006–Present   Inner City Youth Basketball Camp Volunteer
```

Both entries are respectable additions. Ms. Downing has been involved with each of these endeavors for multiple years and her contributions are still ongoing. The resume concludes with "References":

```
REFERENCES

Bill Lawrence
Principal, East High School
(555) 555-5000
blawrence@email.com


Sara Johnson
Principal, Washington Middle School
(555) 555-5550
sjohnson@email.com


Ralph Calhoun
Math Teacher, East High School
(555) 555-5050
rcalhoun@email.com
```

This is just what we would expect from a quality resume. Two supervisors are listed and all three have the contact information listed consistently.

With the exception of the odd header, we have no issues with this document. It is a great representation of Ms. Downing's work and experience. A school in need of a math teacher may find this resume very enticing. Let's see how it stacks up on our resume rubric.

No Educator Left Behind
Resume Rubric

	Fail	Pass
Format	Formatting (font size, font type, punctuation, capitalization, bullets, etc.) is inconsistent	Formatting (font size, font type, punctuation, capitalization, bullets, etc.) is consistent
	Not all mandatory headings (Education, Experience, References) are represented	All mandatory headings (Education, Experience, References) are represented
	White space is inadequate or excessive	White space is appropriate
Education	Education does not meet requirements	Education meets requirements
	Dates are not in a logical order	Dates are in a logical order
	Certifications are not listed	Certifications are listed
Experience	Experience does not meet requirements	Experience does meet requirements
	Dates are not in a logical order	Dates are in a logical order
	Job duties are general and/or irrelevant	Job duties are specific and relevant
Editing	Typographical and/or grammatical errors are present (confirmed by multiple editors)	No typographical and/or grammatical errors are present (confirmed by multiple editors)
	Inaccurate and/or false information	No inaccurate and/or false information
Wording	Weak and/or unprofessional vocabulary	Strong and/or professional vocabulary
	Inconsistent tenses	Consistent Tenses
	Wording is confusing and difficult to read	Wording is clear and easy to read
	An excessive amount of jargon is present	Jargon is not excessive
	Unnecessary information is present	Unnecessary information has been removed
Length	Inappropriate length (three pages or more, plus references)	Appropriate length (one or two pages plus references)
References	References are not listed	References are listed
	References are not listed in a consistent format (name, title, contact information)	References are listed consistently (name, title, contact information)
	No supervisors are listed	Supervisors are listed

Additional Interview Questions

What follows is a continuation of the ten analyzed interview questions from chapter seven. This collection uses the ten strategies presented in that same chapter. There is one question for each strategy (ten questions in total). Because you will likely want more questions to prepare for your interviews, there is an extensive collection available on our website at www.nelb.info.

Question #11: How important is preparation to you?

Quality Response: Some people seem to be able to come and go with the students each day. They are on the same schedule as the bell. I am not one of those people. I take my preparation very seriously and will put in the extra time both at school and at home. I will work hard to create the best possible experience for my students.

What To Watch For: Don't start making excuses as a response to this question. Administrators hate excuses. *"Well, I've got young children at home, so it's hard..."* is not an acceptable response even if it is true. No matter how busy you are, employers want dependable people who don't dance around issues. Additionally, never inquire about contract time during an interview. You can obtain this information elsewhere. If you ask when the end of the contract day is, no matter how good your intentions are the employer will interpret it as, *"How soon can I leave each day?"*

Something To Consider (Strategy #1: Be Specific): You should consider if you have specific answers to each and every question you are asked. Here you may choose to share a story about a time where you were not prepared, what you learned from it and how you have grown from the experience.

Question #12: How do you communicate with parents?

Quality Response: I use all of the more common techniques like newsletters, emails, invitations to classroom events and notes home regarding performance. I am also a big believer in making initial positive contacts. At the beginning of the year I make sure to find something good to share about each child and make a call home to share it with parents. They are typically very excited about getting a positive phone call and if I have to call again later in the year for a negative issue they are more likely to view me as "fair." They will be willing to support me if they know I call for both good and bad reasons.

What To Watch For: Contacting parents can be a difficult and anxiety filled task for some. That doesn't mean that there is an excuse for avoiding it. Parent communication is critical, so don't display unwillingness in your response.

Something To Consider (Strategy #2: Be Memorable): Inquiries about parent communication are common at interviews. If you choose to utilize a portfolio, this could be a wonderful opportunity to present a document that you have used to share information with parents. If you have a stellar weekly memo that you send home each week, make sure to use it as a visual aid as you answer this question.

Question #13: What are your thoughts about Vgotksky's theories?

Quality Response: I believe that if you can keep a student in their Zone of Proximal Development that it will be an immense benefit to their learning. They will acquire new information efficiently without reaching their frustration level.

What To Watch For: This is a dirty question. Not because it is about Vgotsky; we like Vgotsky, he's a good guy from what we understand. With that being said it is highly unlikely that you will be well versed on every single educational theorist. There are far too many of them. So what is one to do if confronted with an unfamiliar name (or concept)? Honesty is the best policy. *"I'm not familiar with his/her work, but I'm a quick learner. I'd be thrilled to learn about any concepts needed to excel at this position."*

Something To Consider (Strategy #3: Show That You've Done Your Homework): Certain districts are huge believers in specific theories or concepts. It could be cooperative learning, multiple intelligences or any number of other possibilities. If you know about these beliefs prior to an interview then you can study them and be prepared.

Question #14: What do you expect of your supervisor?

Quality Response: I would expect them to be honest with me. I am not someone who will be easily offended if there is a problem and would much rather know about it than have it go unsaid. I want a supervisor who will help me to grow each day. This growth will assist me in becoming a more effective educator.

What To Watch For: Don't make it appear as if you are going to be a burden. Your future boss should be there to support you, but you don't want to make it seem as if you are going to be leaning on them constantly.

Something To Consider (Strategy #4: Be Professional): Don't begin listing opinions of what your previous administrators have done wrong. Even if your opinions are justified, it could still be a turnoff to a potential employer. From their vantage point, if you complain about your old boss, you may complain about your new one as well.

Question #15: What is the purpose of consequences?

Quality Response: When I give a consequence it is to educate, not to punish. I'm not looking for retribution. I want them to learn from the situation so it is not repeated.

What To Watch For: Whatever you do, avoid giving an answer that makes it appear as is you are out to "get" kids. No one wants to work with a vengeful person. We are on the same team as the kids; never forget that!

Something To Consider (Strategy #5: Present Well Thought Out Answers): What should you do if you can't think of the appropriate response right away? Take a moment, relax and ask a clarifier to buy yourself some time. *"I believe that sometimes the purpose changes based on a child's individual needs. Are you thinking of a student who regularly receives consequences or one who usually isn't in trouble?"*

Question #16: How do you differentiate instruction?

Quality Response: I've worked with extremely low functioning students, gifted students and every type of student in between. One thing that they all have in common is the ability to learn. You have to find what level the student is functioning at and what assistance they need to progress. Through both formal and informal evaluations you can gather the necessary data to drive instruction at an individual student's level. I use small groups and modified assignments to help meet every students' needs.

What To Watch For: If you are from the old guard that believes that the lower functioning students need to "just work harder" to keep up with their peers, it's time for a change in philosophy. Different students have varying needs. There is no cookie cutter model that will meet them all.

Something To Consider (Strategy #6: Monitor Your Pace): Slow down and take your response to the appropriate level of depth. *"Differentiated instruction is needed. My class uses differentiated instruction every day,"* is not a sufficient answer.

Question #17: Can you tell us about your typical day at work?

Quality Response: I love to get to school early so I can be well prepared for my class. I start the day off by greeting each of my students before the day begins. My students don't respond well to lecture, so I see my role more as a facilitator. I give them enough knowledge to start a project and then I work to keep the learning going. I focus on individual students and assist them as needed. I spend my day connecting with my class as I work to instill a love of learning within each of them.

What To Watch For: This is an ideal opportunity to show that you understand the big picture. While other candidates may be wasting time by giving a step by step breakdown of their day, you can surpass the competition by revealing your style, not your schedule.

Something To Consider (Strategy #7: Give Short And Substantial Answers): A response to this question has the potential to go on indefinitely. No one wants to know that you teach math at 8:05, followed by writing at 9:10 and so on and so forth. Keep it short and powerful.

Question #18: What was the best lesson you have ever taught?

Quality Response: My students were having a difficult time grasping the actual size of the solar system. We decided to create our own scale model for clarification. First we created accurate representations of the planet sizes using paper cutouts. When they got a good look at Mercury in comparison to Jupiter it really blew their minds. The best part was when we took those papers outside to show the relative distance of the planets from one another. We measured out the lengths on an extremely miniature scale. From Venus to Earth took about one step, but when they saw Neptune clear on the other side of the playground it really clicked for them. We went back in and after talking with their groups they wrote a brief paper about what they had learned. Science, math and language arts were integrated into the same lesson and it was very entertaining for all of us.

What To Watch For: Be ready for this question and its opposite, "What is the worst lesson you ever taught?" They are common. You do not want to be stuck thinking through all of the lessons you've ever instructed while trying to determine the best selection.

Something To Consider (Strategy #8: Pay Attention): Be aware of the interviewer. What do you think they want to hear? It is likely that they are searching for someone who can properly describe an engaging lesson based in sound instructional techniques. Give them what they want!

Question #19: How would you handle verbal bullying between students?

Quality Response: Bullying of any nature is unacceptable. Aside from the point that individuals, schools and districts can now be held accountable for civil rights violations when bullying is ignored, the emotional damage done to the targeted student can be immense. I would work to rectify this problem immediately and put measures in place so it would not continue. The students would be questioned, witnesses would be interviewed, documentation would be recorded, stakeholders (parents, administrators, etc.) would be notified, consequences would be assigned and a plan to eliminate this behavior in the future would be established. I will not tolerate bullying.

What To Watch For: Bullying has become a very serious concern in recent years. It is frequently referenced as a precursor to tragedies such as school shootings and suicide. This question warrants a serious answer.

Something To Consider (Strategy #9: Be Proactive): Are you going to create a temporary fix for this situation or a long-term solution? Be proactive and resolve it for now *and* later.

Question #20: How do you feel about getting involved with activities outside of the normal day?

Quality Response: I love contributing at my current school. I am involved with our PTO, after school program, Crisis Team and I volunteer to help at our music programs.

What To Watch For: Don't make excuses or plead ignorance. No one believes *"I want to get involved, but I'm not sure how."* If you haven't been involved up to this point, work to change that. It takes a lot of effort to create a successful school year. If your colleagues have been pulling your weight through committees and opportunities, it's time to step up and contribute.

Something To Consider (Strategy #10: Know Your Resume And Cover Letter): There's no excuse to flounder on this response. If you do, your answer may seem unauthentic. Review what you have been involved in to this point so you are well prepared.

The following page contains a blank Resume Rubric. This is the same rubric that we have been using throughout the book to examine resumes. You are free to copy this rubric for your own personal use. A printable version is also available online at www.nelb.info in the "Resources" section.

The rubric is broken into two separate columns, "Fail" and "Pass." A resume does not always have to achieve a "Pass" in every section to be successful. There is no specific number of "Pass" rankings that need to be received before the resume may be capable of acquiring an interview for the applicant. The only true determination of how polished a resume needs to be is the quality of the other resumes that it will be competing against. With that being said, why leave anything in doubt? You need to make sure that your resume is more impressive than the competition.

Be honest when grading your own resume. Strive to improve it until you are confident that all the criteria fall under the "sufficient" heading. Resume work can be laborious and frustrating, but the time invested is well worth the eventual payoff.

No Educator Left Behind
Resume Rubric

	Fail	Pass
Format	Formatting (font size, font type, punctuation, capitalization, bullets, etc.) is inconsistent	Formatting (font size, font type, punctuation, capitalization, bullets, etc.) is consistent
	Not all mandatory headings (Education, Experience, References) are represented	All mandatory headings (Education, Experience, References) are represented
	White space is inadequate or excessive	White space is appropriate
Education	Education does not meet requirements	Education meets requirements
	Dates are not in a logical order	Dates are in a logical order
	Certifications are not listed	Certifications are listed
Experience	Experience does not meet requirements	Experience does meet requirements
	Dates are not in a logical order	Dates are in a logical order
	Job duties are general and/or irrelevant	Job duties are specific and relevant
Editing	Typographical and/or grammatical errors	No typographical and/or grammatical errors
	Inaccurate and/or false information	No inaccurate and/or false information
Wording	Weak and/or unprofessional vocabulary	Strong and/or professional vocabulary
	Inconsistent tenses	Consistent Tenses
	Wording is confusing and difficult to read	Wording is clear and easy to read
	An excessive amount of jargon is present	Jargon is not excessive
	Unnecessary information is present	Unnecessary information has been removed
Length	Inappropriate length (three pages or more, plus references)	Appropriate length (one or two pages plus references)
References	References are not listed	References are listed
	References are not listed in a consistent format (name, title, contact information)	References are listed consistently (name, title, contact information)
	No supervisors are listed	Supervisors are listed

Synonym Selector

Our Synonym Selector will assist you with taking the vocabulary in your cover letter and resume from vague to vibrant. There are a wide variety of other tools and thesauruses available to assist you. However, this resource is focused on terms that are more specific to resumes. These are some of the most common terms used when describing educational responsibilities.

This tool will help you avoid repetition and say clearly what you want to communicate. You are encouraged to make your own additions as needed. Remember, you want your resume and cover letter to stand out. This is just one more way to help your cause.

Allowed	Began	Determined	Finished
• Approved • Authorized • Certified • Endorsed • Sanctioned	• Assembled • Developed • Installed • Implemented • Proposed	• Analyzed • Assessed • Figured • Examined • Interpreted	• Accomplished • Achieved • Executed • Carried Out • Fulfilled

Handled	Helped	Improved	Led
• Continued • Maintained • Managed • Preserved • Sustained	• Accomodated • Advised • Assisted • Guided • Supported	• Advanced • Enriched • Enhanced • Perfected • Updated	• Chaired • Coordinated • Facilitated • Guided • Monitored

Synonym Selector (continued)

Molded	Organized	Received	Show
• Cultivated • Influenced • Mentored • Motivated • Persuaded	• Arranged • Coordinated • Formulated • Prepared • Scheduled	• Accepted • Acquired • Gained • Honored • Obtained	• Demonstrated • Displayed • Exhibited • Illustrated • Presented

Taught	Wrote	Make Your Own	Make Your Own
• Coached • Educated • Instilled • Instructed • Trained	• Authored • Composed • Created • Drafted • Published		

Trending Topics In Education

The variety of topics that you could be asked about during an interview is limitless; there is no way to prepare for them all. However, having at least a working knowledge of some of the hot topics in our field today will keep you from getting lost should the interviewer inquire about them. We have prepared a list that includes a number of these items. If you find some that you are unaware of then take a moment to do a search online and educate yourself. Preparation is key in the job hunt; don't let the competition outperform you. Please keep in mind that these are only a small portion of the topics that are relevant in our field today. This is by no means a comprehensive list.

504	ability grouping	accommodations
ADD/ADHD	AYP	benchmarks
bilingual education	block scheduling	BOE
cooperative learning	data driven	distance learning
differentiated instruction	ELL/ESL/ESOL/LEP	FERPA
formative assessments	free/reduced lunch	high frequency words
inclusion/mainstreaming	IEP	integrated curriculum
intervention	looping	magnet schools
mandatory reporter	manipulatives	modeling
multiple intelligences	NCLB	norm-referenced
open-ended question	outcomes	pedagogy
PTA/PTO	RTI	scaffolding
sight words	Smart Board	socioeconomic status
state standards	team teaching	validity

(1)

American Association of School Administrators. (2010). Projection of National Education Job Cuts for the 2010-2011 School Year. Retrieved from http://www.aasa.org/uploadedFiles/Policy_and_Advocacy/files/AASAJobCuts0504 10FINAL.pdf

(2)

National Center for Education Statistics. (2009). Digest of Education Statistics 2009. Retrieved from http://nces.ed.gov/programs/digest/d09/

(3)

Career Builder. (2010). Twenty Percent of Workers Plan to Switch Careers/Industries in the Next Two Years. Retrieved from http://www.careerbuilder.com/share/aboutus/pressreleasesdetail.aspx?id=pr544 &sd=1/7/2010&ed=01/07/2010

(4)

Metzger, S. and Wu, M-J (in press). Commercial Teacher Selection Instruments: The Validity of Selecting Teachers Through Beliefs, Attitudes, and Values. *Review of Educational Research.*

(5)

U.S. Census Bureau. (2009). Reported Internet Usage for Households, by Selected Householder Characteristics: 2009. Retrieved from http://www.census.gov/ population/www/socdemo/computer/2009.html

VINCE EVANS

500 E. 24th • Wichita, KS 55500 • 555-555-5500 • nelbbook@gmail.com

EDUCATION

2012   MS, Instructional Design and Technology, Emporia State University

2009   ESL Endorsement, Kansas State University

2007   District Leadership License, Emporia State University

2007   MS, Curriculum and Instruction, Emporia State University

2006   MS, Educational Administration, Emporia State University

2003   BS, Elementary Education, Emporia State University

EXPERIENCE

2009-Present **Principal, Paul B. Cooper Elementary School, Derby, KS**
- Title One Building (94% Free and Reduced Lunch, 60% ESL)
- Obtained Adequate Yearly Progress in both Reading and Math
- Received a Federal Grant worth 2.1 Million Dollars

2007-2009   **Teacher, Allen Elementary School, Wichita, KS**
- Met AYP as a Fourth Grade Teacher
- District Curriculum Task Force Member
- Teachers Networking With Teachers Presenter

2003-2007   **Teacher, Chase County Elementary School, Cottonwood Falls, KS**
- Led Fourth Grade Students to State Standard of Excellence
- Served as Acting Administrator in Principal's Absence
- After School Program Assistant Coordinator

ACTIVITIES

2011-Present Foreign Exchange Student Host

2011-Present Administrator of www.nelb.info

2011   Author of *No Educator Left Behind*

2009-2011   Studied Spanish Abroad in Mexico, Costa Rica and Panama

VINCE EVANS

500 E. 24th • Wichita, KS 55500 • 555-555-5500 • nelbbook@gmail.com

Chris Williams
Superintendant, Derby Public Schools
500 Main Street
Derby, KS 55555
(555) 555-8411
cwilliams@email.com

Hannah Banks
Assistant Superintendant, Derby Public Schools
500 Main Street
Derby, KS 55555
(555) 555-8416
hbanks@email.com

Jane Francis
Board Of Education President, Derby Public Schools
500 Main Street
Derby, KS 55555
(555) 555-8400
jfrancis@email.com

Clint Corby

510 N. Exchange
Haviland, KS 87654
620-555-5452 or 620-555-1111
nelbbook@gmail.com

Relevant Experience

2010-2011   *Superintendent, Mullinville Public Schools*   *Mullinville, KS*
  • Virtual School Administrator   • Guided District Through Consolidation
  • Director of Technology   • Kansas Teacher Evaluation Representative

2007-2011   *Superintendent/Principal, Haviland Public Schools*   *Haviland, KS*
  • 2010 Superintendent of Promise Award   • Developed After School Program
  • Developed Teacher Evaluation Tool   • Testing Coordinator
  • Data Collection System Reporter   • Implemented Four Day School Week
  • Achieved State Standard of Excellence • Challenge Award Recipient

2003-2007   *4th/5th Grade Teacher, Benton Elementary*   *Wichita, KS*
  • Data Coordinator   • Crisis Team Leader
  • Organized Professional Development   • Leadership Team
  • 504 Team Member   • Bus Supervisor
  • Achieved State Standard of Excellence   • Kagan Trainer

Licenses and Certification

State of Kansas District Licensure
State of Kansas Building Leadership K-12
State of Kansas Teacher Certification K-9

Education

2009 District Level Licensure - Friends University
2006 Master of School Leadership - Baker University
2003 Bachelor Degree in Elementary Education - Emporia State University

Community Service

Haviland Play Day Coordinator   After Prom Volunteer
Odyssey of the Mind Regional Judge   County Spelling Bee Moderator

Professional Organizations

Kansas Association of Secondary School Principals   United School Administrators

Out of District Presentations

Beginning Principal Workshop   The Four Day School Week

Activities

Author of *No Educator Left Behind*   Administrator of www.nelb.info

References

Jean Patterson (Board of Education President)
414 E. Main
Anywhere, KS 55550
555-555-5555
jpatterson@email.com

Paul Warkentine (Board of Education Vice President)
318 E. Kingman
Anywhere, FL 55550
555-555-5551
pwarkentine@email.com

John Morgan (Former Supervisor/Superintendent)
205 S. Main
Anywhere, KS 55551
555-555-5552
jmorgan@email.com

Ralph Knott (Former Supervisor/Superintendent)
515 N. Adams
Anywhere, KS 55552
555-555-5553
rknott@email.com

Acknowledgements

*"A good leader takes a little more than his share of the blame,
a little less than his share of the credit.*
~ Arnold H. Glasgow

There is no way that we could have undertaken a pursuit this large without the help of our colleagues. To all of you that have contributed to this effort, you have our sincerest thanks. It is only because of the brilliant and talented people that surround us that this project was possible. Some specific acknowledgments go out to the following people:

Shonda Hayes for suffering through the earliest drafts of this book and helping it to blossom from a garbled mess of notes into its current state. Your willingness to tell us what worked and what didn't was invaluable. Thank you for your devotion to this project.

Heather Corby for helping us to realize that nelb.info was a heck of a lot more catchy than the monstrosity we had in mind.

Marshall Nienstedt for bringing our comics to life. Thank you for sparing the world from our atrocious drawing skills and providing us with many laughs along the way.

Michael Schmidt for taking nelb.info from a concept to a beautifully crafted website. Your assistance in simplifying the technological aspect of this project into something we can easily grasp has been remarkable.

Donnie Hinshaw for the beautiful cover work and website photos. You helped make our vision a reality.

To our feedback team who helped us work through an early draft prior to submitting *No Educator Left Behind* to publishers, Randy and Mary Evans, Cindy and Rick Graves, Rosetta Hayes, Sue Boldra, Danelle Johnson and Katie Swyers, we thank you all.

To all of our colleagues who were willing to share stories from the job hunt and talk shop with us, we appreciate you. Your insight helped to make this book possible.